Grammar and punctuation

Teacher's Resource Book

TERMS AND CONDITIONS

IMPORTANT – PERMITTED USE AND WARNINGS – READ CAREFULLY BEFORE USING

Save for these purposes, or as expressly authorised in the accompanying materials, the software may not be copied, reproduced, used, sold, licensed, transferred, exchanged, hired, or exported in whole or in part or in any manner or form without the prior written consent of Scholastic Ltd. Any such unauthorised use or activities are prohibited and may give rise to civil liabilities and criminal prosecutions.

The material contained on this CD-ROM may only be used in the context for which it was intended in *Scholastic English Skills*, and is for use only by the purchaser or purchasing institution that has purchased the book and CD-ROM. Permission to download images is given for purchasers only and not for users from any lending service. Any further use of the material contravenes Scholastic Ltd's copyright and that of other rights holders.

This CD-ROM has been tested for viruses at all stages of its production. However, we recommend that you run virus-checking software on your computer systems at all times. Scholastic Ltd cannot accept any responsibility for any loss, disruption or damage to your data or your computer system that may occur as a result of using either the CD-ROM or the data held on it.

IF YOU ACCEPT THE ABOVE CONDITIONS YOU MAY PROCEED TO USE THE CD-ROM.

Recommended system requirements:

Windows: XP (Service Pack 3), Vista (Service Pack 2), Windows 7 or Windows 8 with 2.33GHz processor
Mac: OS 10.6 to 10.8 with Intel Core™ Duo processor
1GB RAM (recommended)
1024 x 768 Screen resolution
CD-ROM drive (24x speed recommended)
Adobe Reader (version 9 recommended for Mac users)
Broadband internet connections (for installation and updates)

For all technical support queries (including no CD drive), please phone Scholastic Customer Services on 0845 6039091.

Authors
Huw Thomas and
Christine Moorcroft

Editorial team
Rachel Morgan, Melissa Somers,
Jenny Wilcox, Suzanne Adams,
Red Door Media, Margaret Eaton

Series designers
Shelley Best and Anna Oliwa

Design team
Nicolle Thomas and Andrea Lewis

Illustrations
Gemma Hastilow

CD-ROM development
Hannah Barnett, Phil Crothers and
MWA Technologies Private Ltd

Designed using Adobe Indesign
Published by Scholastic Ltd,
Book End, Range Road, Witney,
Oxfordshire OX29 0YD
www.scholastic.co.uk

Printed by Ashford Colour Press

1 2 3 4 5 6 7 8 9 0   5 6 7 8 9 0 1 2 3 4

British Library Cataloguing-in-Publication Data
A catalogue record for this book is available from
the British Library.
ISBN 978-1407-14067-4

Acknowledgements

The publishers gratefully acknowledge permission to reproduce the following copyright material:

AP Watt at United Agents on behalf of Philip Ridley for the use of an extract from *Kasper in the Glitter* by Philip Ridley (1994, Viking).
Shirley Hughes for the use of an extract from *It's too Frightening for Me!* by Shirley Hughes (1977, Hodder & Stroughton).
Penguin Books for the use of an extract from *Kasper in the Glitter* by Philip Ridley and illustrated by Chris Riddell. Text © 1994, Philip Ridley (Viking 1994, Puffing Books 1995).
United Agents for the use of the poem 'Santa Fe' by Michael Rosen first published in *Mind your own business* (1974, Andre Deutsch).

Every effort has been made to trace copyright holders for the works reproduced in this book, and the publishers apologise for any inadvertent omissions.

Extracts from *The National Curriculum in English, English Programme of Study* © Crown Copyright. Reproduced under the terms of the Open Government Licence (OGL). http://www.nationalarchives.gov.uk/doc/open-government-licence/open-government-licence.htm

Contents

Introduction

Scholastic English Skills: Grammar and punctuation

This series is based on the premise that grammar and punctuation can be interesting and dynamic – but on one condition. The condition is that the teaching of these grammar aspects must be related to real texts and practical activities that experiment with language, investigate the use of language in realistic contexts and find the ways in which grammar and punctuation are used in our day-to-day speech, writing and reading. This book encourages children to look back at their written work and find ways to revise and improve it.

Teaching grammar and punctuation

'As a writer I know that I must select studiously the nouns, pronouns, verbs, adverbs, etcetera, and by a careful syntactical arrangement make readers laugh, reflect or riot.'

Maya Angelou

The *Scholastic English Skills: Grammar and punctuation* series equips teachers with resources and subject training to enable them to teach grammar and punctuation effectively. The focus of the resource is on what is sometimes termed 'sentence-level work', so called because grammar and punctuation primarily involve the construction and understanding of sentences.

Many teachers bring with them a lot of past memories when they approach the teaching of grammar. Some will remember school grammar lessons as the driest of subjects, involving drills and parsing, and will wonder how they can make it exciting for their own class. At the other end of the spectrum, some will have received relatively little formal teaching of grammar at school. In other words, there are teachers who, when asked to teach clause structure or prepositions, feel at a bit of a loss. They are being asked expectantly to teach things they are not confident with themselves.

Grammar can evoke lethargy, fear, irritation, pedantry and despondency. Yet as demonstrated by the above comment from Maya Angelou, even one of our greatest modern writers presents her crafting of sentences as an exciting and tactical process that has a powerful effect on her readers. Can this be the grammar that makes teachers squirm or run?

About the product

The book is divided into six chapters. Each chapter looks at a different aspect of grammar and punctuation and is divided into sections. Each section includes teachers' notes – objective, background knowledge, notes on how to use the photocopiable pages, further ideas and digital content – and up to three photocopiable pages.

Posters

Each chapter has two posters. These posters are related to the contents of the chapter and should be displayed and used for reference throughout the work on the chapter. The poster notes (on the chapter introduction page) offer suggestions for how they could be used. There are black and white versions in the book and full-colour versions on the CD-ROM for you to print out or display on your whiteboard.

Activities

Each section contains three activities. These activities all take the form of a photocopiable page which is in the book. Each photocopiable page is also included on the CD-ROM for you to display or print out (answers are also provided, where appropriate, in a separate document on the CD-ROM).

Many of the photocopiable pages have linked interactive activities on the CD-ROM. These interactive activities are designed to act as starter activities to the lesson, giving whole-class support on the information being taught. However, they can also work equally well as plenary activities, reviewing the work the children have just completed.

Workbooks

Accompanying this series is a set of workbooks containing practice activities which are divided into chapters to match the teacher's resource book. Use a combination of the photocopiable pages in this book and the activities in the workbook to help children practise and consolidate grammar and punctuation skills.

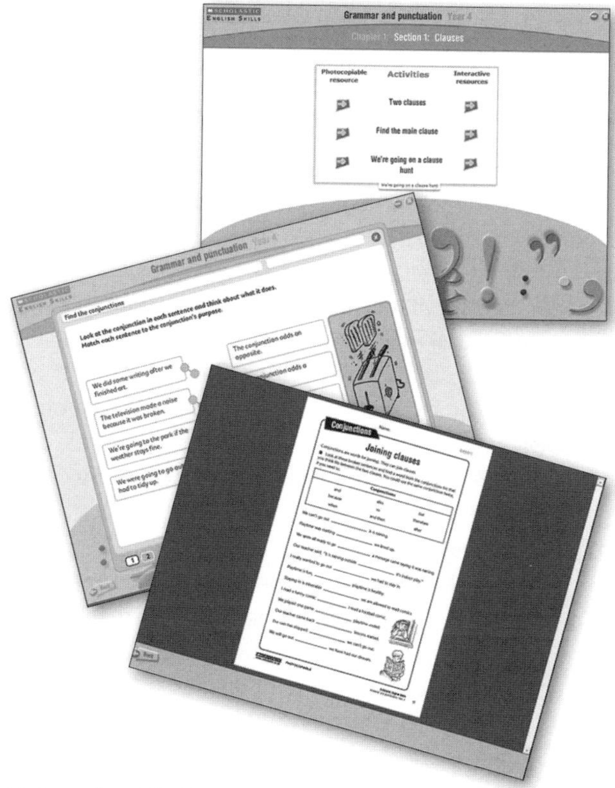

Using the CD-ROM

Below are brief guidance notes for using the CD-ROM. For more detailed information, see 'How to use this CD-ROM' on the Main menu.

The CD-ROM follows the structure of the book and contains:

- All of the photocopiable pages.
- All of the poster pages in full colour.
- Answers provided, where relevant.
- Interactive on-screen activities linked to the photocopiable pages.

Getting started

Put the CD-ROM into your CD-ROM drive.

- For Windows users, the install wizard should autorun, if it fails to do so then navigate to your CD-ROM drive. Then follow the installation process.
- For Mac users, copy the disk image file to your hard drive. After it has finished copying double click it to mount the disk image. Navigate to the mounted disk image and run the installer. After installation the disk image can be unmounted and the DMG can be deleted from the hard drive.
- To install on a network, please see the ReadMe file located on the CD-ROM (navigate to your drive).

To complete the installation of the program you need to open the program and click 'Update' in the pop-up. Please note – this CD-ROM is web-enabled and the content will be downloaded from the internet to your hard-drive to populate the CD-ROM with the relevant resources. This only needs to be done on first use, after this you will be able to use the CD-ROM without an internet connection. If at any point any content is updated you will receive another pop-up upon start up with an internet connection.

Main menu

The main menu is the first screen that appears. Here you can access: terms and conditions, registration links, how to use the CD-ROM and credits. To access a specific year group click on the relevant button (NB only titles installed will be available). To browse all installed content click **All resources**.

Chapter menu

The Chapter menu provides links to all of the chapters or all of the resources for a specific year group. Clicking on the relevant Chapter icon will take you to the section screen where you can access the posters and the chapter's sections. Clicking on **All resources** will take you to a list of all the resources, where you can search by keyword or chapter for a specific resource.

Section menu

Here you can choose the relevant section to take you to its activity screen. You can also access the posters here.

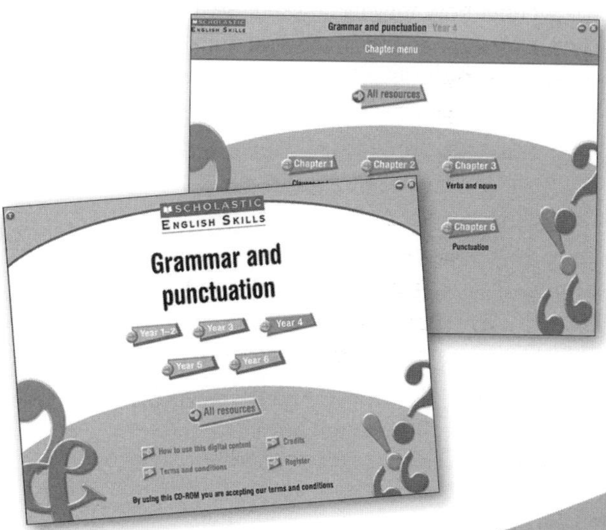

Activity menu

Upon choosing a section from the section menu, you are taken to a list of resources for that section. Here you can access all of the photocopiable pages related to that section as well as the linked interactive activities.

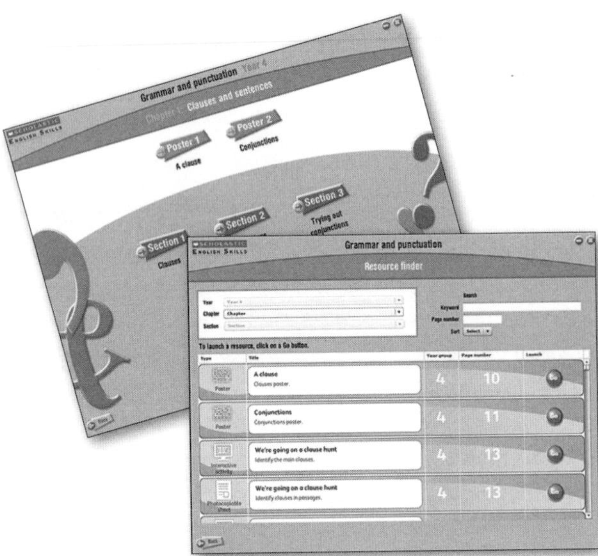

All resources

All of the resources for a year group (if accessed via a Chapter menu) or all of the installed resources (if accessed via the Main menu). You can:

- Select a chapter and/or section by selecting the appropriate title from the drop-down menus.
- Search for key words by typing them into the search box.
- Scroll up or down the list of resources to locate the required resource.
- To launch a resource, simply click on the **Go** button.

Navigation

The resources (poster pages, photocopiable pages and interactive activities) all open in separate windows on top of the menu screen. To close a resource, click on the **x** in the top right-hand corner of the screen and this will return you to the menu screen.

Closing a resource will not close the program. However, if you are in a menu screen, then clicking on the **x** will close the program. To return to a previous menu screen, you need to click on the **Back** button.

Teacher settings

In the top left-hand corner of the Main menu screen is a small **T** icon. This is the teacher settings area. It is password protected, the password is: login. This area will allow you to choose the print quality settings for interactive activities 'Default' or 'Best'. It will also allow you to check for updates to the program or re-download all content to the disk via **Refresh all content**.

Answers

The answers to the photocopiable pages can be found on the CD-ROM in the All resources menu. The answers are supplied in one document in a table-format, referencing the page number, title and answer for each relevant page. The pages that have answers are referenced in the digital content boxes on the teachers' notes pages. Unfortunately, due to the nature of English, not all pages can have answers provided because some activities require the children's own imaginative input or consist of a wider writing task.

Objectives

	Page	Section	English skills objective	To extend the range of sentences with more than one clause by using a wider range of conjunctions, including when, if, because, although.	To use the present perfect form of verbs in contrast to the past tense.	To choose nouns or pronouns appropriately for clarity and cohesion and to avoid repetition.	To indicate possession by using the possessive apostrophe with singular and plural nouns.	To use the forms 'a' or 'an' according to whether the next word begins with a vowel.	To know the grammatical difference between plural and possessive 's'.	To use standard English forms for verb infections instead of local spoken forms.
Chapter 1	12	Clauses	Revisit clauses.	✓						
	16	Conjunctions	Understand the way in which clauses can be linked using conjunctions.	✓						
	20	Trying out conjunctions	Identify and use an increasing range of conjunctions in writing.	✓						
	24	More than one clause	Write sentences with more than one clause, using a range of conjunctions.	✓						
	28	Experimenting with clauses in writing	Apply knowledge about clauses and linking clauses to writing.	✓						
Chapter 2	35	Apostrophes to show possession	Revisit the use of apostrophes in singular and plural nouns to signify possession.				✓			
	39	Possession in plural nouns	Use apostrophes accurately to mark plural possession in nouns.				✓			
	43	Plural and possessive 's'	Understand the difference between plural and possessive 's'.				✓		✓	
	47	Possessive pronouns	Understand the purpose of, and identify, possessive pronouns.			✓				
	51	Developing possession in writing	Secure the use of possessive apostrophes and possessive pronouns in writing.			✓	✓		✓	
Chapter 3	58	Verbs and verb tenses	Revisit verbs and verb tenses.		✓					
	62	How verbs change	Become aware of standard English forms for verb inflections.		✓					✓
	66	Using verbs correctly	Use standard English forms for verbs.							✓
	70	Nouns and determiners	Begin to understand the function of determiners and how they are used in writing.					✓		
	74	Writing with accuracy	Use verbs, nouns and determiners consistently and accurately in writing.		✓			✓		✓

Objectives

	Page	Section	English skills objective	To choose nouns or pronouns appropriately for clarity and cohesion and to avoid repetition.	To use conjunctions, adverbs and prepositions to express time and cause.	To use fronted adverbials.	To use commas after fronted adverbials.	To use and punctuate direct speech.	To use paragraphs as a way to group related material and organise around a theme.	To use headings and subheadings to aid presentation.	To use noun phrases expanded by the addition of modifying adjectives, nouns and prepositional phrases.
Chapter 4	81	Noun phrases	Consider how noun phrases can be expanded.								✓
	85	Expanding noun phrases	Expand noun phrases in writing.								✓
	89	What is an adverbial?	Understand what an adverbial is and identify adverbials in texts.			✓					
	93	Using adverbials	Begin to use adverbials in writing.			✓	✓				
	97	Developing sentences	Develop sentences by using expanded noun phrases and adverbials in writing.			✓					✓
Chapter 5	104	Nouns and pronouns	Revisit nouns and pronouns and their functions in sentences.	✓							
	108	Choosing nouns and pronouns	Choose nouns and pronouns to aid clarity and cohesion and avoid repetition.	✓							
	112	Using paragraphs in writing	Use paragraphs to organise ideas around a theme.						✓		
	116	Organising sentences and texts	Consider how sentences and texts are organised.						✓	✓	
	120	Cohesion in writing	Write clearly and cohesively within sentences and across paragraphs.	✓					✓	✓	
Chapter 6	127	Revisiting punctuation	Identify and consolidate understanding of basic punctuation.	Revision of previous years' knowledge.							
	131	Direct speech	Revisit the use of inverted commas to indicate direct speech.					✓			
	135	Punctuating direct speech	Punctuate direct speech correctly.					✓			
	139	Adverbials and commas	Use a comma after an adverbial that precedes a verb.			✓	✓				
	143	Using a range of punctuation in writing	Apply punctuation accurately in writing.			✓	✓	✓			

Chapter 1

Clauses and sentences

Introduction

This chapter consolidates the children's learning about clauses and conjunctions: a clause is a group of words, including a verb, which can act as a sentence; a conjunction is a word or group of words acting together, which can be used for joining clauses (or words or phrases). Children learn to recognise and use an increasing range of conjunctions and use them in their writing, as they decide whether a short or long sentence is more appropriate. For further practice, please see the 'Clauses and sentences' section of the Year 4 workbook.

In this chapter

Poster notes

A clause (page 10)
It can be difficult to give a clear definition of a clause. The poster gives a working definition. There will be exceptions to the rule and a whole host of elements are taken under the general category of 'words linked to that verb'. However, the verb is the important thing for children to look for in their delineating of clauses within sentences – as is emphasised on this poster.

Conjunctions (page 11)
The poster lists words that can act as conjunctions. These words play a vital role in the construction of longer and more complex sentences. The poster will be a useful reference point to help children to identify conjunctions in texts. As they learn to identify conjunctions by their role in sentences, children will be able to add others to the poster. It will also be useful in suggesting conjunctions that they might use in their writing.

Vocabulary

Children should already know:
statement, question, exclamation, command, clause, main clause, conjunction
In Year 4 children need to revisit:
how to express time, place and cause using conjunctions; the terms 'clause', 'main clause' and 'conjunction'

Clauses and sentences

A clause

A clause is a group of words that includes a verb.

Some sentences have just one clause:

Nobody swam in the pool.
The shark got there first.

Some sentences have more than one clause:

a clause — **Nobody swam in the pool**
another clause — **because the shark got there first.**

Clauses and sentences
Conjunctions
unless
after
but
then
however
because
when
also
or
therefore
so
so that
and
before

Clauses

Objective

Revisit clauses.

Background knowledge

Clauses are units of language that make sense in themselves. They can be whole sentences, such as *The dog barked*, or can feature within sentences. Within sentences they feature as distinct elements with verbs of their own. In a sentence like *The dog barked and the cats purred*, there are two distinct clauses:

- *The dog barked, the cats purred.*

This sentence has two main clauses about two different actions. In a sentence like *The dog barked because it was excited*, there are also two clauses:

- *The dog barked, it was excited.*

This time, the main clause (*The dog barked*) is followed by a clause that provides information about the dog barking, and is therefore a subordinate clause.

In both sentences each clause could make a discrete, short sentence.

Activities

- **Photocopiable page 13 'We're going on a clause hunt'**

This activity reminds the children what a clause is. It asks them to find the clauses in a story about children who themselves are hunting for clauses in an everyday situation. Remind them that a clause is a group of words that has a verb and that might make sense as a sentence. Some of the sentences have one clause, and others have two. For differentiation, where a sentence has two clauses children can look for words that link them. Some children could also write their own sentences with two clauses and identify these and any words that link them. Point out that the word 'so' links the two clauses in the first sentence.

- **Photocopiable page 14 'Two clauses'**

In this activity children are asked to separate the two clauses in a sentence. Remind them that one way of doing this is by locating the verbs. Remind them that clauses are like mini-sentences. After completing the activity, they can look at the ways in which some clauses are subordinate to others.

- **Photocopiable page 15 'Find the main clause'**

This is a paired activity in which children work together to find the main clauses of sentences. Next they examine the rest of the sentences to identify another clause that depends on the main clause for sense – a subordinate clause. In each sentence they could also identify words/groups of words that link the two clauses – conjunctions – and discuss how these affect the meanings of the sentences.

Further ideas

- **The most clauses:** Children can look at texts available in the classroom with the challenge of trying to find the sentence that contains the greatest number of clauses (and identifying each of those clauses).
- **Clause consequences:** Group the children according to attainment. Ask them to write a sentence that has two clauses on a strip of paper, so that they can cut it in half to separate these clauses. They should number them 1 or 2 on the back to show their order in the sentence, and then make two sets: 1s and 2s. For a more challenging activity, ask some groups to write a sentence in which one clause is more important than the other (a main and a subordinate clause). They write 'main' or 'subordinate' on the back and split them into their two sets. Ask them to repeat this, writing more sentences. They place the clauses face down and take turns to pick up one from each set and read out the sentence they make. They could end up with humorous sentences such as:
  - *The dog barked to buy a dress.*

Digital content

On the digital component you will find:

- Printable versions of all three photocopiable pages.
- Answers to all three photocopiable pages.
- Interactive versions of all three photocopiable pages.

Clauses

We're going on a clause hunt

- Read the passage, including the notices.
- Underline the clauses in each sentence. The first one has been done for you.

<u>It was a bright sunny day</u> so <u>Mum said she'd take us out</u>. We were going to the beach but there would be one condition. What was that?

"You're not allowed to say that you're bored!"

Jake and I just looked at one another because we never get bored at the beach. In the car Mum gave us a task. It was quite a surprise but we put our mobile phones away. The task was a clause hunt!

"Look around. Listen to everything. Spot a clause and write it down. I'll check your answers when we get to the beach. Here's a pad and pencil each."

This was going to be like school, but we didn't argue about it. Around town there were loads of signs and notices.

Special offers! Order your laptop before it's too late!	**Last chance!** Buy now or you'll miss a great bargain!	**Please phone to make an appointment with our financial advisor**

There were market traders shouting out clauses.

> Come in and try our pies. You'll never find better unless there's a 'z' in the month.

> Have a cup of tea, and then come back for another.

> We sell the freshest fish that swim round our coast. Buy quickly before they swim home.

Name:

Two clauses

- Each of these sentences contains two clauses.
- Write each clause in the spaces underneath the sentence.

The car stopped because it ran out of petrol.

After we finished dinner, we went out to play.

Ahmed is seven today so we are having a party.

I like lemonade but my mum can't stand it.

Name:

Clauses

Find the main clause

A sentence can have two or more clauses that are equally important:

The cat slept and the kittens played.

The two main clauses are

The cat slept	the kittens played

A sentence can also have two or more clauses, with one – the main clause – being more important than the others. The main clause is the main thing the sentence is about. Less important clauses are called subordinate clauses:

The cat slept | because she was tired.

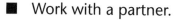

- Work with a partner.
- Underline the main clauses in these sentences in green.
- Underline the subordinate clauses in blue.

Tip: Look for the verbs.

I fed the dog because she was hungry.

Our dog barks when the postman comes.

He gives dogs biscuits so that they will be friendly to him.

He has been scared of our neighbour's dog since it bit him.

He doesn't go into the garden when it's there.

Our neighbour doesn't get his mail unless he keeps his dog indoors.

When our cat saw the biscuits he jumped onto the postman's shoulder.

The postman doesn't bring our mail if he sees the cat.

Conjunctions

Objective

Understand the way in which clauses can be linked using conjunctions.

Background knowledge

Conjunctions link units of language (such as words, phrases or clauses). There are two types of conjunction: 'coordinators' and 'subordinators' (children do not need to learn these terms). Coordinators (such as 'and', 'but', 'or') link units of equal status and introduce an addition, opposition or alternative. Subordinators are mainly used to introduce subordinate clauses. There are many more subordinators than coordinators for introducing subordinate clauses that relate in different ways to the main clause, for example: time ('when', 'then', 'after'), reason/cause ('because', 'so', 'so that'), condition ('unless', 'if').

Activities

- **Photocopiable page 17 'Joining clauses'**
The sentences can be completed using the conjunctions supplied. Point out that a conjunction can be one word, or two or more words that work together. Some conjunctions will need to be used more than once, but encourage the children to choose as wide a variety as possible. Afterwards they could consider what each conjunction does: add information ('and', 'also'), add an opposite idea or a contrast ('but'), say when something happens ('when', 'and then', 'after') or why ('so', 'therefore', 'because').
- **Photocopiable page 18 'Choose the conjunction'**
As they create sentences using the parts shown on the photocopiable sheet, children have to consider the most appropriate conjunction to link two clauses. This will involve understanding the relationship between the two clauses and finding an appropriate word. Note that this activity introduces the conjunction 'or' for linking two main clauses as alternatives.
- **Photocopiable page 19 'Find the conjunctions'**
Using their awareness of the different functions performed by conjunctions, children work in pairs to identify the conjunction in each sentence, think about what the conjunction does and then match a description to the sentence.

Further ideas

- **Find other ones:** Looking through various texts, children find new conjunctions and list them in a table according to the function they perform.
- **Conjunction challenge:** Challenge the children to produce a sentence that uses four different conjunctions.
- **Conjunction survey:** Children carry out a survey of the most commonly used conjunctions in any text they have been reading, for example: each child could check a different page of a story the class has read and note how many examples there are of 'and', 'but', 'or' and so on.

Digital content

On the digital component you will find:

- Printable versions of all three photocopiable pages.
- Answers to all three photocopiable pages.
- Interactive versions of 'Joining clauses' and 'Find the conjunctions'.

Joining clauses

Conjunctions are words for joining. They can join clauses.

■ Look at these broken sentences and find a word from the conjunctions list that you think fits between the two clauses. You could use the same conjunction twice, if you need to.

Conjunctions		
and	also	but
because	so	therefore
when	and then	after

We can't go out ________________ it is raining.

Playtime was starting ________________ we lined up.

We were all ready to go ________________ a message came saying it was raining.

Our teacher said, "It is raining outside ________________ it's indoor play."

I really wanted to go out ________________ we had to stay in.

Playtime is fun, ________________ playtime is healthy.

Staying in is miserable ________________ we are allowed to read comics.

I read a funny comic ________________ I read a football comic.

We played one game ________________ playtime ended.

Our teacher came back ________________ lessons started.

The rain has stopped ________________ we can't go out.

We will go out ________________ we have had our dinners.

Name:

Conjunctions

Choose the conjunction

- Look at the sentence parts below. Choose starters, conjunctions and finishers that fit together and make sentences. Write them below.
- Make up your own sentences using a starter, a conjunction and a finisher.

Starters	Conjunction	Finishers
We could play football	but	I had my tea.
First I went home	and	the water had boiled.
I went to the park	also	we could play cricket.
I set out for school	after	my friend came.
We went to the fair	then	she moans too much.
Our teacher is grumpy	so that	I could buy a new game.
I saved my pocket money	because	I had finished my breakfast.
The steam came out of the kettle	or	the roller coaster was closed.

Conjunctions

Find the conjunctions

Conjunctions are words or phrases that can link clauses in different ways.

- Work with a partner.
- Shade the conjunction in each sentence.

We did some writing after we finished art.
The television made a noise because it was broken.
We're going to the park if the weather stays fine.
We were going to go out but we had to tidy up.
The children lined up before going into school.
The hinges are loose so the door won't open.
Don't cross the road unless it's safe.
We plan to look at the stars when it gets dark.
Ella goes swimming or plays football on Saturdays.
The water boiled and the toast popped out of the toaster.

- Think about what the conjunction does in each sentence. Cut out the boxes and match them to the sentences.

The conjunction…

…adds information: and, also	…adds an opposite: but, although
…adds an alternative: or	…adds a condition: if, unless
…adds a condition: if, unless	…says when something happens: then, when, after, before
…says when something happens: then, when, after, before	…says when something happens: then, when, after, before
…says why something happens: so, so that, because, to	…says why something happens: so, so that, because, to

Trying out conjunctions

Objective

Identify and use an increasing range of conjunctions in writing.

Background knowledge

The meaning of a sentence can be changed by changing a conjunction, for example: *We can go to the cinema and visit the museum* has a different meaning to *We can go to the cinema or visit the museum*. In the first sentence, the conjunction 'and' adds information (the sentence means that we can do both activities) while 'or', in the second, gives an alternative (we can only do one or the other). *I went home when it got dark* has a different meaning to *I went home because it got dark*. In the first sentence, the conjunction 'when' simply tells us when the person went home, whereas 'because' means that the darkness caused the person to go home.

Activities

- **Photocopiable page 21 'Conjunction collection'**
As an initial stimulus to looking at the variety of conjunctions for joining clauses, this activity asks children to list some varied examples found in different texts. If using disposable texts they could cut out the examples and add them to a class collection. Look for patterns in the purposes of conjunctions used in each type of text.
- **Photocopiable page 22 'Use the conjunction'**
This activity presents conjunctions with different purposes that children can use to connect their own clauses to make sentences.
- **Photocopiable page 23 'Complete the sentence'**
By finishing the sentences, children have to consider the content of the first clause but they also have to look at the conjunction and assess where it is leading the sentence. They will notice that some of the sentences are identical up to the point where the conjunction is added. It will be interesting to compare the way in which different conjunctions lead to different clauses.

Further ideas

- **Analysing leaflets:** Collect information leaflets from a variety of sources and ask children to read through them to find the different conjunctions that are used to join clauses.
- **Text marking:** Using leaflets and cuttings, children can find conjunctions and circle them, then draw lines from the circled conjunctions to the clauses they join together.
- **Text changing:** Provide a text whose meaning can be changed by altering some of the conjunctions between clauses. A non-fiction text, such as instructions or an explanation could be changed in this way to produce something humorous.

Digital content

On the digital component you will find:

- Printable versions of all three photocopiable pages.

Name:

Trying out conjunctions

Conjunction collection

■ Collect a variety of texts – for example, newspapers, leaflets, packaging, recipe books, games instructions…

■ Find the conjunctions used to link words in these texts.

Text	Conjunctions
"Safe Crossing" road safety poster	then before but and

Name:

Trying out conjunctions

Use the conjunction

■ Write a sentence that has two clauses. Use each conjunction in the table.

Conjunction	Sentence
so that	We will switch on the heating so that we can be warm.
because	
then	
also	
if	
unless	
or	
therefore	
when	
but	
although	

Name:

Trying out conjunctions

Complete the sentence

■ Look at these sentences. Write a clause to complete each sentence.

We waited for the bus and ______________________________

____

I am going to visit my friend although ______________________________

____

Sam wrote a letter because ______________________________

____

We waited for the bus but ______________________________

____

We are planning a game of football once ______________________________

____

We planned a game of football so ______________________________

____

I am going to visit my friend unless ______________________________

____

We waited for the bus until ______________________________

____

Sam wrote a letter when ______________________________

____

I am going to visit my friend while ______________________________

____

More than one clause

Objective

Write sentences with more than one clause, using a range of conjunctions.

Background knowledge

A single-clause sentence can be short, for example: *Ten bottles were standing on the wall.* However, more information can be added to it without adding another clause: *Ten dark green bottles with gold tops were standing upright on the old drystone wall in the moonlight*. A multi-clause sentence can be fairly short (for example, *The ten bottles were on the wall when the sun set*) but can also be very long: *Ten bottles were on the wall when the sun set, but when the moon rose they had gone, so I fetched a torch and went to look for them*. The same information can be communicated by linking clauses in different orders or using different conjunctions:

- *As the sun set there were ten bottles on the wall; however they had gone by the time the moon rose, so I fetched a torch and went to look for them.*
- *I fetched a torch and went to look for the ten bottles that had been on the wall when the sun set but had gone by the time the moon rose.*

Children should learn that sentences can have one, two or more clauses, but need not learn the terms 'single-clause' and 'multi-clause'.

Activities

- **Photocopiable page 25 'Two sentences into one'**
Once children have remodelled their sentences, they can compare the changes they made. Afterwards they can compare the different conjunctions they used to communicate the same meaning.
- **Photocopiable page 26 'Short and long sentences'**
Drawing on a selection of short, single-clause sentences, children are asked to create longer, multi-clause sentences. One aspect of this activity worth following up is the use of conjunctions. Children will use different conjunctions, depending on the relationship between the clauses.
- **Photocopiable page 27 'Build long sentences'**
This paired activity requires children to create humorous sentences by linking the clauses provided. Encourage them to think about the conjunctions they use – would a different one improve the sentence or change the meaning?

Further ideas

- **Change conjunctions:** Children can look through different texts for multi-clause sentences and identify the conjunctions linking the clauses. They can then try replacing the conjunctions with others for different effects.
- **Sentence shuffle:** Children can try making their own sets of clauses like the ones used on photocopiable page 27 'Build long sentences'. They will probably need no encouragement to write clauses with potential humour to provide opportunities for very funny multi-clause sentences.
- **The longest:** Using the conjunctions featured in these activities, children can try building the longest sentence with the greatest number of conjunctions, for example: *Before we thought about what we were going to write, we wrote this long sentence because our teacher set us the challenge, but she said that we wouldn't be able to do it, so we couldn't resist.* It is important to discuss whether a long sentence or multiple shorter ones is the more effective in different contexts.

Digital content

On the digital component you will find:

- Printable versions of all three photocopiable pages.
- Answers to 'Two sentences into one'.

More than one clause

Two sentences into one

You can take two short sentences:

It was raining.	Playtime was indoors.

and use a different conjunction to turn them into one sentence, for example:

It was raining so playtime was indoors.

or:

Playtime was indoors because it was raining.

■ Find two different ways to turn these sets of two sentences into one sentence. The meaning must be the same each time.

Luke's clothes were wet.	He fell in the pond.

My shoes were dirty.	I cleaned them.

The water boiled.	Gran made a cup of tea.

■ Make up some of your own pairs of short sentences.
■ Join them in two ways to make long sentences.

Name:

More than one clause

Short and long sentences

■ Look at these short sentences.

We are not happy.	We helped the lunch supervisors.	We will show our parents.	We are working together.
We can't go outside.	We have nearly finished.	We are making a display.	We cooperated.
We have to tidy up.	The bell rang.	We are working very hard.	We go to lunch.
Our teacher asked us to help.	We didn't finish our work.	We are enjoying ourselves.	We finished our work.
It is raining outside.	We are practising a play.	We finished our pictures.	We are waiting for the bell.

■ Use these short sentences as clauses in longer sentences. Try using two short sentences to make each long sentence. You can use any conjunctions you need to link the clauses, for example:

We helped the lunch supervisors until the bell rang.

Name:

More than one clause

Build long sentences

- Work with a partner.
- Use the clauses below to make up some long and strange sentences – for example, *My dog fell off the wall because Granny's teeth fell out.*
- Use conjunctions to link the clauses.
- Put in the correct punctuation for each sentence.

my dog fell off the wall	the burglar ran away
my mum was sad	they met at a cafe beside the sea
they went all over the table	she spun round and round
she saw a cat	Granny's teeth fell out
she lost at them at Cleethorpes	he ate a bowl of cornflakes
he scratched his neck	scare away midges
she woke up in the middle of the night	Aunty Louisa sneezed
ate a jam sponge	I fell in the pool
the clock struck twelve	he was wearing a pair of bright green trunks
he wouldn't get caught	she started to cry

Experimenting with clauses in writing

Objective

Apply knowledge about clauses and linking clauses to writing.

Writing focus

Building on previous activities on clauses, this section encourages children to improve individual sentences in their writing by reflecting on, and experimenting with, their use of clauses.

Skills to writing

These activities develop children's understanding of how different types of sentence are used to suit different types of text. The children investigate sentences in different text types and notice patterns in the numbers of clauses used and the conjunctions used to link them.

- **Conjunctions in varied texts**

Look out for the jobs being done by conjunctions in different texts. For example, children might notice that stories and non-fiction recounts use conjunctions that signal time to a greater extent than, say, arguments, persuasive texts, advertisements and promotional texts. They will probably find that explanations make greater use of conjunctions signifying reasons and causes, and so on. They can use what they learn to help them to use appropriate types of sentence in their own writing.

- **Focus on the clause**

The clause is one of the most important tools for developing children's writing. From a basic sentence, they can develop a connection that elaborates their expression in writing. Children need to get used to looking at simple sentences and asking whether more could be added.

- **Two sentences or one**

Look out for examples where two short sentences could be combined to form one extended sentence – as on photocopiable page 25 'Two sentences into one'. Also point out that there are times when two short sentences are more appropriate than one longer one, perhaps to create a specific effect. Children could investigate this by taking a section of text that has short, single-clause sentences and rewriting it in a way that links sentences with conjunctions, or vice versa. Ask them what difference this makes and why the author wrote it as he/she did. Ask children to look for 'two to one' possibilities in their own writing and to decide which is better – one long or two short sentences.

Activities

- **Photocopiable page 30 'Investigating sentences'**

Split the children into groups and give each group samples of a different type of text to investigate, for example: newspaper reports, instructions, explanations, non-fiction books on events in history, promotional leaflets, guides to places (for example castles, stately homes, museums or other sites). Some of these could be printed, others online. Ask children to read different sections of the texts and choose typical sentences to investigate. Afterwards they can compare their findings with those of other groups and discuss what they notice about the types of sentence used and the conjunctions linking the clauses in different types of text. Each group could pick out the sentence with the most clauses in their text and read it aloud or display it on the whiteboard. If another group has a sentence with more clauses they read it out/display it, and so on.

- **Photocopiable page 31 'Connecting ideas'**

This photocopiable sheet helps children to focus on the conjunctions they use in their writing. It can be used with any pieces of writing they do. Children can then compare the different conjunctions that are useful in different types of writing, and discuss why, for example: 'then' is useful in recounts; 'because' helps with explanations; 'so' and 'therefore' are commonly used in arguments and persuasion.

Write on

- **Sentence strips**

Children can select sentences from a their own writing and copy them on a long strip of paper. They can then cut these up to change a word, insert a conjunction and add a clause to extend the sentence.

- **Excuses**

Ask the children to imagine that this morning everyone was late for school. Using the conjunctions on poster page 11, ask them to write excuses that are elaborate and imaginative – and impress the angry teacher by using the full range of conjunctions: *On the way to school something happened, and then something else, and just then... and after that....* Once they have written up these paragraphs of imaginative tales, children can practise saying them to the teacher, who should try to look serious, as if believing the excuses. For inspiration, try reading Jill Murphy's *On the Way Home* (Macmillan Children's Books), a classic story.

- **Sentence marathon**

Begin with a short sentence and challenge the children to take turns to add a clause to it, each time repeating what has gone before. You could record it as you go, to remind any who forget the previous part of the sentence. Sample starter sentences: *Mrs Patel bought a car*; *Mr Jones went to town*; *The horse ambled across the field*; *The cat leaped onto the wall*; *The lorry was rolling down the hill*; *A spaceship landed in our garden*.

Digital content

On the digital component you will find:

- Printable versions of both photocopiable pages.

Name:

Experimenting with clauses in writing

Investigating sentences

This is an investigation into the number of clauses in sentences within different texts.

- Work in groups.
- Each group investigates a different type of text.
- Choose three sample sentences from each text. Count the number of clauses in each sample. Make a note of one of the sentences.
- What have other groups discovered?

Text title	Type of text	Number of clauses in sentence	Sample sentence

Name:

Experimenting with clauses in writing

Connecting ideas

- What are you writing about?

- What type of text is it?

- Tick the conjunctions you think will be the most useful for joining clauses.
- Use these in your writing. If you use others, tick those, too, but in a different colour.
- Add any others you used at the bottom.

and	also	as well	but
however	or	so	so that
because	therefore	in order to	to
when	then	after	before
meanwhile	if	unless	in case

Chapter 2

Possession

Introduction

In this chapter the children revisit the use of apostrophes to indicate possession in singular nouns, looking at how the apostrophe follows the noun and precedes the letter 's' that is added to indicate possession: *the cat's ears*, *the girl's book*, *a man's hat*, *Amy's house*. They learn how to use apostrophes to indicate possession for plural (including irregular) nouns: *the cats' ears*, *the girls' books*, *the men's hats*, *the children's house*. For further practice, please see the 'Possession' section of the Year 4 workbook.

Poster notes

Apostrophes for possession (page 33)
This poster can be used for revision of singular possessives and to help learn the rules for showing possession with plural nouns. Use the buses image to explore how the plural is made possessive (add the apostrophe after the 'es'). Use this rule for other regular plurals ending 'es', for example: 'foxes', 'boxes'. Similarly, look at how the possessives of 'goose' and 'geese' are formed and use the rule to form possessives of other irregular plurals that do not end with 's' or 'es', such as 'men', 'women', 'children', 'sheep', and so on.

Pronouns for possession (page 34)
The text and actions on this poster could be used as the basis for a simple enactment, with children using different objects in the classroom, for example books: *This book belongs to me. It is my book. It is mine. That book belongs to him/her. It is his/her book. It is his/hers.* It can also be displayed as a reminder of the different types of possessive pronouns and how to use them, including their spellings – notably that they never contain apostrophes ('ours', 'hers', 'its', 'theirs').

In this chapter

Vocabulary

Children should already know:
apostrophe
In Year 4 children need to know:
pronoun, possessive pronoun

Possession

APOSTROPHES FOR POSSESSION

The car's wheels

The cars' wheels

The bus's wheels

The buses' wheels

The goose's feet

The geese's feet

The mouse's tail

The mice's tails

Possession

Pronouns for possession

Apostrophes to show possession

Objective

Revisit the use of apostrophes in singular and plural nouns to signify possession.

Background knowledge

These activities provide revision of previous learning in Years 2 and 3 about the use of apostrophes to signify possession. It is important to remind children not to add an apostrophe when making a noun plural.

Apostrophes can be used to show possession. An apostrophe near the end of a noun can show that it possesses an item that follows it (*Sean's book*). Rules for adding apostrophes depend on the endings of the nouns to which they are being added.

- If the noun is singular and doesn't end with the letter 's', add an apostrophe then 's': *Sam's gerbil*.
- If the noun is singular and ends with 's', add an apostrophe then 's': *Ross's cat*.
- If the noun is plural and doesn't end with 's', add an apostrophe then 's': *the children's dog*.
- If the noun is plural and ends with 's', add an apostrophe but don't add 's': *the babies' rattles*.

Activities

- **Photocopiable page 36 'Find the possessive apostrophes'**

The story contains eight apostrophes that indicate possession. Children identify these and use the table to show what the apostrophe tells us, using the format *the… belonging to…* (*the neighbour's hillside – the hillside belonging to the neighbour*). The children could then rewrite some of the whole sentences containing apostrophes in this format, or in the format *the… of the…*, on a separate sheet of paper.

- **Photocopiable page 37 'Noun grid'**

The grid looks at the way nouns are classified when apostrophes are added. Children cut out the nouns shown and sort them on to the Carroll diagram, matching the column and row to place nouns correctly. After sorting the nouns in this way they can write (on a separate piece of paper) a sentence that shows something belonging to each noun, applying the correct possessive ending, for example: *Kate's bike has a red saddle*, *The geese's beaks are yellow*.

- **Photocopiable page 38 'Santa Fe'**

This complicated poem is made comprehensible by its apostrophes. The children are asked to make sense of the action in the fourth, fifth and sixth stanzas. One way of doing this would be to write the characters' names – Cook, Turkey and Jelly – next to the ones the poet uses. They can then figure out who is eating whom!

Further ideas

- **Dictation:** Children could listen to a page of a story that contains apostrophes that denote possession, spot these and write them down. Remind them not to use apostrophes to form plurals.
- **A trail of possession:** Write a 'progressive' narrative to display on the whiteboard for children to take turns to add a new noun with possessive apostrophe: *Tess's cat jumped onto the wall, because it was chased by Billy's dog. The dog has eaten Charlie's chocolate….*
- **Nursery-rhyme possessions:** Ask children to identify apostrophes of possession in nursery rhymes. They can then write complete sentence answers to questions such as *Whose horses and men couldn't fix Humpty Dumpty? (All the horses and men belonging to the king) Whose sheep got lost?*, and so on.

Digital content

On the digital component you will find:

- Printable versions of all three photocopiable pages.
- Answers to all three photocopiable pages.
- Interactive versions of 'Find the possessive apostrophes' and 'Noun grid'.

Apostrophes to show possession

Find the possessive apostrophes

■ Look at this piece of writing and highlight the apostrophes that show possession.

One day a shepherd took his sheep to his neighbour's hillside. One lamb could not keep up. A wolf sneaked up and grabbed the lamb's leg. The lamb noticed the whistle in the wolf's pocket.

"Do not eat me," she said. "I cannot die without a send-off."

The wolf was puzzled.

"Please play your whistle," she said. "I shall do a little dance for my funeral and then you can eat me."

Even more puzzled, the wolf agreed.

He played and the lamb danced, but the shepherd's dogs heard the whistle's sound and chased the wolf away. The wolf realised the lamb's trick.

"That will teach me a lesson," he said. "I have been tricked into doing a musician's work instead of a wolf's job."

Based on a fable by Aesop

■ Now write the words with apostrophes in the table. Explain what each apostrophe tells us. The first one has been done for you.

Word	**What the apostrophe tells us**	**Word**	**What the apostrophe tells us**
neighbour's hillside	the hillside belongs to the neighbour		

Apostrophes to show possession

Noun grid

■ Cut out the words at the bottom of the page and sort them into the Carroll diagram below.

	Does not end in 's'	Ends in 's'
Singular		
Plural		

Kate	Ross	Mr Harris	woman	geese	Paris	mice
fishes	women	dogs	coats	Sam	people	dog

Name:

Apostrophes to show possession

Santa Fe

■ Look at the poem. Try to work out what is happening. Write notes alongside stanzas 4, 5 and 6.

Three clues:
the 'Hobbler' is the cook,
the 'Gobbler' is the turkey,
the 'Wobbler' is the jelly.

It was a stormy night
one Christmas day
as they fell awake
on the Santa Fe

Turkey, jelly
and the ship's old cook
all jumped out
of a recipe book

The jelly wobbled
the turkey gobbled
and after them both
the old cook hobbled

Gobbler gobbled
Hobbler's Wobbler.
Hobbler gobbled
Wobbler's Gobbler.

Gobbly-gobbler
gobbled Wobbly
Hobbly-hobbler
Gobbled Gobbly.

Gobbler gobbled
Hobble's Wobble
Hobble gobbled
gobbled Wobble.

gobble gobble
wobble wobble
hobble gobble
wobble gobble

from *Mind Your Own Business* by Michael Rosen

Possession in plural nouns

Objective

Use apostrophes accurately to mark plural possession in nouns.

Background knowledge

Plural possession in nouns is indicated using an apostrophe. In regular plurals the apostrophe follows the letter 's': *the dogs' kennels, the girls' toilets, the babies' mothers*. In irregular plurals that do not end with 's', the apostrophe precedes the 's' that is added to indicate possession: *the men's clothing shop, the people's opinions, the children's nursery*.

Activities

- **Photocopiable page 40 'Placing apostrophes'**

This activity begins with a review of the rules for using the apostrophe. Children use these rules to help them to place apostrophes in the possessive words to match the context of the sentences.

- **Photocopiable page 41 'Apostrophes in sentences'**

The children add an apostrophe and, where appropriate, the letter 's' to form the possessive forms of plural nouns as they use them in sentences.

- **Photocopiable page 42 'The owners' apostrophes'**

This requires the children to think about the information in the picture and accompanying brief text to decide who owns the item depicted and whether the owner is singular or plural. They then use their knowledge of the rules for adding apostrophes to help them to write a very short sentence saying who owns what. The final example provides an opportunity for a more complex answer (either *It is the mice's cage* or *It is Jeremy's mice's cage*).

Further ideas

- **Book title ownership:** The children could add the missing apostrophes to book, story or poem titles and write sentences to say who owns what in titles such as *Charlottes Web*; *Alices Adventures in Wonderland*; *Joe Giants Missing Boot*; *Harry Potter and the Philosophers Stone*; *Carries War*; *The Oathbreakers Shadow*; and *Jinxs Magic*.
- **What's the title?:** Provide book titles in disguised form and ask the children to write them as they would appear on the books, for example: *The new frock belonging to Bill*; *The midnight garden of Tom*; *The Fairy Tales of the Grimms*; *The Travels of Gulliver*; and *The Fables of Aesop*.
- **Singular to plural:** Ask children to convert singular possessive phrases to plural: *the country's capital* (*the countries' capitals*), *the teacher's computer, the cat's tail, the goose's neck, the man's jacket, the sheep's fleece*. Remind them to check they have the correct plural form before they add the possessive apostrophe, and 's' if appropriate.

Digital content

On the digital component you will find:

- Printable versions of all three photocopiable pages.
- Answers to 'Placing apostrophes' and 'The owners' apostrophes'.
- Interactive version of 'Placing apostrophes'.

Name:

Possession in plural nouns

Placing apostrophes

Here are the rules for the use of apostrophes.

If the noun is singular and doesn't end with 's' add an apostrophe then an 's', for example: *Sam's dog.*	If the noun is singular and ends with 's' add an apostrophe then 's', for example: *Ross's dog* *Paris's tower.*
If the noun is plural and doesn't end with 's' add an apostrophe then 's', for example: *the children's dog* *the mice's cage.*	If the noun is plural and ends with 's' add an apostrophe but *don't* add 's', for example: *the babies' rattles* *the teachers' mugs.*

■ Add apostrophes to these sentences.

I went to Ellies house to play football with her older twin brothers new goal posts. Ellie kicked the ball wide and it smashed the Mosses window. We went to say we were sorry and offered to pay the neighbours bill. We had a shock when we found out the glaziers price for fixing one window. It was more than two weeks pocket money.

Ellies brother James told us that we should play with dolls instead. Jamess opinion was that that football was a mens game. We said it was a girls game, too. Their mum added that it was a womens game as well.

After that we went indoors to clean out the fishes tank.

Name:

Possession in plural nouns

Apostrophes in sentences

■ Look at this list of owners.

princess	men	leopard	people
mice	children	babies	cook
cows	hippopotamuses	firefighter	prime minister

■ Think of an item that could belong to each owner. Write a sentence about something they own. Use an apostrophe to show that they own this.

 Name:

Possession in plural nouns

The owners' apostrophes

■ Answer each question with a sentence. Don't forget the apostrophes.

Whose chair is it?	Whose bib is it?	Whose mug is it?
It is the __________s chair.	It is __________ __________.	__________ __________.
Whose toilet is it?	Whose house is it?	Each stable is for a pony. Whose stables are they?
__________ __________.	__________ __________.	__________ __________.
Whose pen is it?	Whose car park is it?	Whose cage is it?
__________ __________.	__________ __________.	__________ __________.

Plural and possessive 's'

Objective

Understand the difference between plural and possessive 's'.

Background knowledge

The apostrophe joined the English language from French in the 16th century and its usage spread from contraction to possession. It is now often incorrectly used, sometimes being inserted before any 's' ending: *Carpet's at bargain prices, fish and chip's*. (In the first case, its use wrongly suggests that something belongs to a carpet rather than that there is more than one carpet for sale.) At the other extreme, the apostrophe has dropped out of usage in many contexts, deemed to be unnecessary as the job it would be doing can often be gauged from the context – such as in product logos and signs. But its use is inconsistent – for example, it features on Levi's jeans but has been dropped from Waterstones in recent years.

Activities

- **Photocopiable page 44 'In the plural'**

This activity reminds children how to form plurals and that a plural never has an apostrophe unless it also shows possession. It is useful to remind children of their previous learning about nouns. When they rewrite the sentences, they could begin by highlighting all the nouns and making them into plurals. They might also need to change verbs and pronouns to match – this also consolidates previous learning.

- **Photocopiable page 45 'The apostrophe police'**

Here the children help 'the apostrophe police' to eliminate unnecessary apostrophes from a news report.

- **Photocopiable page 46 'Usage survey'**

The children are asked to survey the usage of the apostrophe, looking at restaurant names in particular. This involves them in an aspect of language that is undergoing change, as the apostrophe drifts out of use in a number of contexts. Let the activity lead in to a discussion of the usefulness of the apostrophe.

Further ideas

- **Uses around us:** Ask the children to look out for uses of the apostrophe in shop or market displays, signs and notices. They may notice examples where the apostrophe has been misused, or where one is missing.
- **Bad apostrophes:** Collect examples of incorrect use of apostrophes on signs, menus and so on for the children to discuss and to identify where apostrophes would be used in correct grammar.
- **Signs with apostrophes:** Photograph road signs and place names with apostrophes or with names that could, but do not all, have apostrophes, for example: *St John's Road*, *King's Cross*, *St James's Palace*, *Lords cricket ground*, *Golders Green*. The children could explain how these follow the rules on poster page 33 'Apostrophes for possession' or how they do not follow the rules, and how to correct them. They could also compare place-name signs with apostrophes with their spellings on maps and notice any differences. Children could photograph their own examples to contribute to a classroom display 'The phantom apostrophe'.

Digital content

On the digital component you will find:

- Printable versions of all three photocopiable pages.
- Answers to 'In the plural' and 'The apostrophe police'.
- Interactive version of 'The apostrophe police'.

Name:

Plural and possessive 's'

In the plural

■ Plural means more than one. Write the plurals of these words.

drum ____________ piano ____________ stitch ____________

quiz ____________ path ____________ puppy ____________

You don't need an apostrophe to form a plural.

If you used any apostrophes just for making plurals, correct your answers now!

■ Rewrite these sentences in the plural. The first one has been done for you.

Anna bought a comic.

Anna bought some comics.

The horse galloped around the field.

____

The man watched the helicopter landing.

____

Anna's brother plays chess.

____

The dog's kennel was very expensive.

____

I am going to see my cousin's new baby.

____

The car went right through Mr Potts's flower bed.

____

Plural and possessive 's'

The apostrophe police

■ Read the report below and highlight any words that have apostrophes that are not needed.

■ Write them in the cell. The first one has been done for you.

Yesterday the city's police officers' arrested more than twenty word's lurking in the food department of Spark's and Fencer – each clutching an unnecessary apostrophe. Shoppers' anger made them report the rogue words' to sales' staff.

"We are only allowed apostrophe's for possession and not for plural's," said Ima Snitch, 42. "So, why should shop's get away with extra one's?"

Spotting the police, the rogue word's tried to hide behind the cabbage's. They were big cabbage's but the officers' eagle eyes' didn't miss a thing. Soon, to everyone's relief, the apostrophe's were all behind bar's awaiting trial.

We would like to add that other store's also sell cabbage's.

Plural and possessive 's'

Usage survey

The apostrophe is sometimes used too much.

Or it is not used when it could have been.

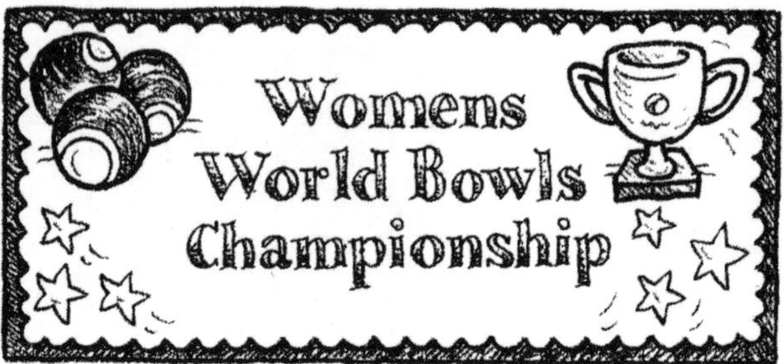

- Use a photocopy of a column of restaurants from the telephone directory. Stick it in the blank column on the right-hand side of this page.
- Put a circle around the restaurants that name the owner.

How many could have used an apostrophe but don't?

How many do use an apostrophe?

- Look at other sections of the phone book or at local shop signs and try to find examples of 'left-out' apostrophes.

Possessive pronouns

Objective

Understand the purpose of, and identify, possessive pronouns.

Background knowledge

Remind the children of their previous learning about pronouns and how they are used. Use the poster on page 33 to explain how we use possessive pronouns.

Note that some possessive pronouns are used with a noun (*that is my hat*) and others can stand alone (*that is mine*). The exception is 'its', which is usually used with a noun (*the river has burst its banks*).

Possessive words used attributively (that is to say, before the noun), are also known as 'possessive adjectives', or 'possessive determiners', since they modify the noun. This category includes words such as 'my', 'your', 'his', 'her' and so on. Possessive pronouns never have apostrophes.

Person	Singular	Plural
First	my, mine	our, ours
Second	your, yours	your, yours
Third	her, hers his (used with or without a noun) its	their, theirs

Activities

- **Photocopiable page 48 'Possessive pronoun match'**

The mixing of personal and possessive pronouns in this activity leads children to try matching sentences in which the two types of pronoun correspond. The children should say the sentences aloud to check they sound right. Once they have successfully matched the sentences, they could underline the possessive pronouns.

- **Photocopiable page 49 'Possessive pronouns'**

This activity focuses on how we use pronouns to show possession. It is useful first to remind the children of how we use pronouns instead of nouns to avoid repetition. At this point the term 'possessive pronouns' can be introduced for pronouns that show ownership and that can be used instead of nouns with 'possessive' apostrophes. Look together at these two sentences:

- *I saw James today and James was riding James's new bike.*
- *I saw James today and he was riding his new bike.*

Explain that we don't need to repeat 'James' because it is clear who 'he' is and to whom 'his' refers – so the second sentence is less clumsy. Display poster page 34 'Pronouns for possession' and emphasise that possessive pronouns never have apostrophes. Then display some sentences on the whiteboard for the children to change nouns to pronouns, as appropriate, such as: *Tom gave Alice an apple. Alice thanked Tom for the apple. Alice ate the apple and told Tom it was very sweet.*

- **Photocopiable page 50 'Possessives'**

Through reflecting on the people referred to in this activity, children should fall back on the possessive pronouns and adjectives they know to find the right word to begin each of the sentences. Gender and whether there is one or more will indicate the correct pronoun.

Further ideas

- **Matching:** Children can write the name of a person or group of people on one card and a sentence about them on another. In the sentence they can try using a possessive pronoun. They can then try producing two different cards, choosing anyone as the subject, provided their choice leads them to use different pronouns.

Digital content

On the digital component you will find:

- Printable versions of all three photocopiable pages.
- Answers to Possessive pronoun match' and 'Possessive pronouns'.
- Interactive version of 'Possessive pronoun match'.

Name:

Possessive pronoun match

- Cut out the sentences below.
- Try matching the sentences on one side of the page with the ones on the other side of the page. The result will be two sentences that fit together.
- Stick the matching sentences on a separate sheet of paper.

This bike belongs to me.	They are theirs.
This book belongs to you.	It is his.
That coat belongs to him.	They are hers.
This football belongs to her.	They are ours.
This house belongs to them.	They are mine.
This television belongs to us.	They are his.
These stickers belong to me.	It is hers.
These crayons belong to you.	It is ours.
These sandwiches belong to him.	It is yours.
These shoes belong to her.	It is mine.
These sweets belong to them.	They are yours.
These flowers belong to us.	It is theirs.

Possessive pronouns

- We can use possessive pronouns to show ownership (possession).
- Possessive pronouns never have apostrophes.

This bike belongs to me. It is my bike. The bike is mine.

This bike belongs to her. It is her bike. The bike is hers.

Those bikes belong to them. They are their bikes. The bikes are theirs.

- Read the speech bubbles above. The first sentence in each one has been written in two different ways. Rewrite the sentences below in two different ways using possessive pronouns.

This house belongs to us. ______________________________

____

The book belongs to you. ______________________________

____

Mr and Mrs Rose own that house. ______________________________

____

She owns all those pencils. ______________________________

____

The bat belongs to him. ______________________________

____

That chair belongs to me. ______________________________

____

 Name:

Possessive pronouns

Possessives

■ Look at the sentences below. Think about the people referred to in each sentence. Complete the sentence, filling in the possessive pronoun and writing the end of the sentence. The first one has been done for you.

About me	**About my friend**
My task is finding missing words.	________ name is ________
About my school ________ classrooms are ________	**About our teachers** ________ staff room is ________
About me and my friend ________ favourite game is ________	**About my bedroom** ________ floor is ________
About our head teacher ________ favourite day of the week is ________	**About me** ________ favourite pop song is ________

■ Try some possessive sentences of your own about other people. It could be people in your family or people in your street.

Developing possession in writing

Objective

Secure the use of possessive apostrophes and possessive pronouns in writing.

Writing focus

Building on previous activities, this section encourages children to refine their use of punctuation to indicate possession, and helps them consider their use of possessive pronouns in writing.

Skills to writing

- **Newspaper apostrophes**

Hunt and define the use of the apostrophe for possession in printed texts. Give the children copies of a newspaper article and ask them to work in groups to highlight as many as they can. Invite feedback from each group while the others listen carefully and check whether these apostrophes really show possession or are being used for another purpose (for example, to show a contraction) – or even appear by mistake, as misprints.

- **Lost apostrophes**

Display a short text on the whiteboard with the apostrophes that show ownership deleted. Invite the children to make sense of it by taking turns to read a sentence aloud and add the apostrophes.

- **Who owns what?**

Display a poem or a chapter of a story written on the whiteboard and ask the class to read it to themselves and to notice any possessive pronouns in it. They could highlight these and say what these tell the reader (Who owns what?). They could then carry out a similar activity using a printed copy of another text, explaining what each possessive pronoun tells us.

Activities

- **Photocopiable page 53 'Apostrophes for owners'**

Ask the children to use what they have learned about apostrophes to help them to rewrite the passage, replacing phrases that show ownership with nouns that have apostrophes to show possession/ownership. They could continue the story, paying attention to apostrophes.

- **Photocopiable page 54 'Pronouns for owners'**

Ask the children to use what they have learned about possessive pronouns to help them to rewrite the information in each speech bubble, replacing phrases that show ownership with possessive pronouns. They could then write some examples of their own.

Write on

- **Story titles**

Kit's Wilderness and *Uncle Montague's Tales of Terror* are two examples of story titles that include possession. The children could use the idea as a way of creating interesting story ideas of their own. To add a challenge, why not insist on alliteration. What, for example, might lie behind *The Count's Curtain* or in *The Beefeater's Bin-Bag?*

- **In the jackdaw's nest**

Begin by showing a picture of a jackdaw and explaining that these birds have a reputation for picking up shiny objects and taking them to their nests. You could read the poem 'The Jackdaw of Rheims' by Richard Harris Barham (1788–1845), which can easily be found on the internet. Children could use apostrophes to describe ownership of items the jackdaw in the poem stole and to list them. Ask the class to contribute lines to a shared poem about the contents of a jackdaw's nest, using apostrophes to show who owned each item it collected. The objects could be too big for the nest and involve the jackdaw building an extension – any humorous ideas the children come up with.

- **Lost property**

Give the children a list of ten items from a 'lost property cupboard', such as a clockwork fish that sings when wound up, a small meteorite, a brooch in the shape of a peacock, a book on beekeeping, a shovel, a bunch of roses, a screwdriver, a magnifying glass and a calculator. They invent characters who own each item, using possessive pronouns to express ownership, and work in groups to tell a story about how they lost these items and how they and the characters become connected. They can then write their own versions of the story, taking care to spell the possessive pronouns properly and not to use apostrophes in them.

Digital content

On the digital component you will find:

- Printable versions of both photocopiable pages.
- Answers to both photocopiable pages.
- Interactive version of 'Apostrophes for owners'.

Developing possession in writing

Apostrophes for owners

■ Rewrite this passage using apostrophes to show possession. The first sentence has been done for you.

The parents of Anna went to meet the head teacher of the school of the witches. The name of the head witch was Mrs Spell. When they arrived the father of Selima was also waiting to see Mrs Spell. Mrs Spell showed the parents of the children around the school.

She stopped at the door of the Year 4 class and said, "I'll introduce you to the sorcerer of the Year 4 class. The name of the sorcerer is Professor Fizz."
Then she showed them the magic garden of the older children, the library of the school, the classrooms of the other year groups and the broomstick parking area for parents.

Mrs Spell asked if the parents of the children had any questions. The mother of Anna asked if children had to wear the uniform of the school. Mrs Spell said, "The choice belongs to you but I think the capes of the children create the right atmosphere."

Anna's parents went to meet the head teacher of the witches' school. ____________

Name:

Developing possession in writing

Pronouns for owners

■ For each speech bubble, write a sentence using a possessive pronoun. The first one has been done for you.

1. That spaceship is mine.
2. __________
3. __________

4. __________
5. __________
6. __________

Chapter 3

Verbs and nouns

Introduction

This chapter consolidates children's previous learning about how verbs work in sentences. It provides practice in using different forms of verbs in the past and present tenses, including auxiliary verbs and irregular forms. Children have opportunities to consider different shades of meaning and different effects of verbs with similar meanings and to make effective choices in their writing. For further practice, please see the 'Verbs and nouns' section of the Year 4 workbook.

Poster notes

Verbs past and present (page 56)
This reminds children of the different ways in which verbs change for the past and present tenses. For each verb they could suggest another that changes in a similar way from present to past tense, for example: **'turned'**, 'asked', 'talked', 'walked', 'opened', 'jumped'; **'stopped'**, 'clapped', 'skipped', 'pinned'; **'changed'**, 'raced', 'used'; **'find'/'found'**, 'wind'/'wound', 'bind'/'bound'; **'think'/'thought'**, 'bring'/'brought'; **'sink'/'sank'**, 'drink'/'drank', 'stink'/ 'stank'; **'know'/'knew'**, 'grow'/'grew', 'throw'/'threw'; **'tell'/'told'**, 'sell'/'sold'.

Determiners (page 57)
This poster introduces determiners. The children will already be well aware of words such as 'a', 'an', 'the', 'this', 'that', 'those', 'these' and so on, which introduce noun phrases. Here children learn how determiners clarify meaning.

In this chapter

Vocabulary

Children should already know:
verb, adverb, tense (past, present)
In Year 4 children need to know:
present perfect

Verbs and nouns

Verbs past and present

Present			Past		
turn	stop	change	turned	stopped	changed
win	go	come	won	went	came
find	write	draw	found	wrote	drew
think	sink	know	thought	sank	knew
make	take	tell	made	took	told
sell	fall	leave	sold	fell	left

Verbs and nouns

Determiners

Here are some determiners: **a an the**

We use determiners with nouns to say whether the listener or reader knows about the noun.

A determiner begins a noun phrase. Here are some more determiners:

this **that** **those** **any** **all** **no** **every**

Verbs and verb tenses

Objective

Revisit verbs and verb tenses.

Background knowledge

Verbs are words that express a tense and an action or state of being. This can be a feeling, such as 'like', 'prefer', 'hope', 'wonder'. The present tense expresses an action or state of being that is going on now. Different forms of the present tense express different meanings: *I go to the high school* implies a habitual action; *I am going to the high school* could mean that I am on my way to the high school or that I will go to the high school at some time in the future. Words such as 'am', 'is', 'will', 'might', 'can' and 'should' are auxiliary verbs (children do not need to know this term), which can change the meanings.

The past tense can be expressed by changing the verb or adding an auxiliary verb. Many verbs can be converted to the past tense by adding 'ed' (if necessary, modifying the ending of the root word). Others have irregular past tenses: 'go'/'went', 'run'/'ran', 'eat'/'ate', 'fly'/'flew', 'freeze'/'froze'. The formation of the past tense creates different meanings:

- *She went to the cinema* suggests an event that has happened and is over.
- *She was going to the cinema* suggests an event that may or may not have happened, or could precede a clause beginning with a conjunction such as 'when', 'after' or 'because'.
- *She has gone to the cinema* suggests an event that has happened but is still going on.
- *She has been going to the cinema* suggests a recurring event.

Activities

- **Photocopiable page 59 'Verbs in action'**

Children can use this photocopiable sheet to identify verbs in sentences they collect from different texts. They should notice that every sentence has a verb. If they can't find any verbs in the 'sentence', point out that this means it is not, in fact, a sentence. This is also an opportunity to revisit clauses, children could also look for the clause containing each verb.

- **Photocopiable page 60 'Possibilities'**

The children choose two possible verbs that could complete a sentence. They could share their answers with others, reading their sentences aloud and comparing the different effects of the verbs they chose.

- **Photocopiable page 61 'Magazine extracts'**

This activity presents 'magazine' extracts indicating the past, present or future time. The children identify the verbs, some of which are made up of more than one word. Before they begin it is useful to demonstrate the use of auxiliary verbs to write about events that are happening now, or in the past, or are going to happen in the future: *would pop in*, *can stand*, *will need*. Sometimes the auxiliary verb can be separated from the main verb by another word: *can **happily** stand*. The children can describe how the verbs change to show when something happens.

Further ideas

- **Verb-pops:** A list of popular verbs can be maintained in the classroom. It can be a list of ten verbs encountered in stories that grabbed the interest of the children. They can nominate and vote on candidates for the list and alter it every so often.
- **Slang verbs:** Using selected sources, children listen to spoken language in which verbs are formed using non-standard English, for example: *I were just going out when…*, *We was right here….* They identify the non-standard verb formations and say how to change them for formal speech/writing.

Digital content

On the digital component you will find:

- Printable versions of all three photocopiable pages.
- Answers to 'Magazine extracts'.
- Interactive version of 'Magazine extracts'.

Verbs and verb tenses

Verbs in action

■ Look at different texts such as newspapers, leaflets, packages and so on. Cut out eight sentences and glue them onto the table. List the verbs.

■ Decide whether each sentence can make sense without any verbs.

INSTRUCTIONS Open the green packet and remove the nuts and bolts.	Open remove

Name:

Verbs and verb tenses

Possibilities

■ For each of the sentences below, list two possible verbs. Try to think of some powerful ones or some unusual ones. The first one has been done for you.

The dog	ran fled	from the burning house.
I		round my room to find shoes.
The baby		because he was hungry.
The spaceship		into space.
The thief		when he saw the police car.
A firework		in the sky.
The mountain climber		onto the ledge.
My gran		when she is in a bad mood.
The monster		out of the cave.
I dropped a glass and it		.

Name:

Verbs and verb tenses

Magazine extracts

- Highlight the verbs and verb phrases in these texts.
- Note when each event happens: present, past or future.

Queen Sweep

Pop group Sweeper flew in to London this week to receive their 'London Hits' award for best group. They also won the award for 'Best song' and came second in the 'Best video' category. But the band were more interested in other things. "We wanted to see the Queen," lead singer Sam told reporters. "Yeah! We thought it would be cool and that she would pop into the party. She probably went to the wrong place."

When? ______________________

Widdering Heights

The news is out. Singer Phil Widders, pop's wild child, is scared of something. Phil tells us he hates tall buildings. "I hate heights," he says, "but it is a strange sort of fear. I can happily stand on a tall building. I hate it when I stand outside one and look up at the top. It terrifies me." Oooooh.

When? ______________________

Pop group Buzz have another hit with this one. Many say it is their best song ever. It features in the hit film *Slides* and includes guitarist Matt doing a violin solo!

When? ______________________

New single from Mice Girls

Record shops will need space outside the doors on 14 July. The new Mice Girls single will be released on that date. The girls will fly into London for the release and will appear on the roof of 'Majestic Records' in the city, where they will perform the single for fans.

When? ______________________

How verbs change

Objective

Become aware of standard English forms for verb inflections.

Background knowledge

A verb inflection is the change made to a verb to make it agree with its subject or to alter its tense. For example, *I walk*, *I go* (first person singular verbs, present tense), change to *he walks, he goes* (third person singular, present tense): the endings 's' and 'es' are added to make the verbs agree with the subject 'he'. To change *I walk* to the past tense, the ending 'ed' is added to give *I walked*; when *I go* is changed to the past tense, a whole new word is used: *I went* ('go' is an irregular verb).

In standard English verbs agree with their subjects, although this is not always the case in colloquial usage, for example: *I seen him*, *We was at school*, *He were at our house*, *He should have went*. These vary according to region and are perfectly clear to listeners, and in some settings seem more natural than their standard English forms. It is important that children are aware of this and able to use standard English in their writing. It is also important not to denigrate regional usage that has developed over generations.

Activities

● **Photocopiable page 63 'Verb pairs'**
This activity involves children in matching past- and present-tense verbs. They could also glue the two columns they make onto a large sheet of paper in order to compare them side by side and so that they can add others. Afterwards, ask the children to separate the verbs that have past tenses formed by adding 'ed' and to look at how the past tense is formed in the remaining verbs ('stop'/'stopped' – double the consonant before adding 'ed'; 'swim'/'swam' – a new word is formed by changing the vowel, and so on).

● **Photocopiable page 64 'Tense changer'**
Here the children are asked to change verbs from past to present or present to past tense. Ask them to use just one word for each verb (*I cut* rather than *I was cutting*). Ask them to make sure that the verb matches the person doing it ('I'). Afterwards, the children could make notes about whether the words would be different if the person doing each verb was 'he' or 'she' instead of 'I'.

● **Photocopiable page 65 'Into the past'**
This activity presents a humorous passage in which the verbs in brackets are in the infinitive form. The children write the verbs in the past tense, using the most appropriate form each time. They may need help changing some irregular verbs into the past tense ('put'/'put', 'hear'/'heard', 'hang'/'hung', 'lie'/'lay').

Further ideas

● **Pass the sentence:** Play this game in which immediate responses are required: Children take turns to say a very short sentence in the present tense (*I jump*), then pass it on. The next speaker says the same thing in the past tense (*I jumped*). The first speaker then puts the sentence back into the present tense but in a different form (*I am jumping* instead of *I jump*). Finally the second speaker repeats it in a different form of the past tense (*I was jumping…* instead of *I jumped…*).

● **Altering tenses:** Use sentences from stories set in the past and retell them in the present or future, noticing how the verbs change.

● **Big change/Little change:** Focus on the nature of the alteration made to verbs when they switch from present to past tense. Remind children that verbs such as 'I walk' just have the 'ed' morpheme added to make 'walked', while some verbs (like 'I am') change completely ('I was'). Ask if children can think of any verbs in the work they have done that do not change at all ('put', 'cut').

Digital content

On the digital component you will find:

- Printable versions of all three photocopiable pages.
- Answers to 'Tense changer' and 'Into the past'.
- Interactive version of all three photocopiable pages.

Name:

How verbs change

Verb pairs

■ Cut out the verbs below. Can you find a present tense and past tense of the same verb? Place them alongside each other.

■ When you have finished make up some pairs of your own.

watched	shout	stop	bit	see
wrote	find	ran	play	won
type	walked	helped	swam	stopped
run	made	win	ate	walk
shouted	help	write	saw	bite
found	eat	typed	draw	played
swim	drew	make	watch	

Name:

How verbs change

Tense changer

■ Complete this grid. You need to change the past-tense verbs into present tense and the present-tense verbs into past tense.

■ Can you think of some other verbs and their different tenses? Make a list on the back of this sheet.

Past	Present
I slid	
I lived	
	I am
	I do
	I cut
I said	
	I hide
I chased	
	I freeze
	I hear
I ate	
	I change
I chose	
	I blow
I sprang	
	I learn
I stopped	
I fell	
I clung	
	I work
I opened	
	I leap
I thought	
I told	
	I feel
I trekked	

Name:

How verbs change

Into the past

- The verbs in this passage are in brackets.
- Write them in the past tense.
- You can use whichever form of the past tense you think is right each time but it must match the person doing it. The first one has been done for you.

Jake's mum, Mrs Blake, (to say) ______said______ that Tilly the cat (to need) ____________ an anti-worm tablet. This (to be) ____________ bad news for the cat. Tilly (to hate) ____________ any type of tablet. So Mrs Blake (to wrap) ____________ Tilly in a towel, (to open) ____________ the cat's mouth and (to put) ____________ the tablet right at the back of her tongue. Tilly (to hiss) ____________, (to scratch) ____________ Mrs Blake's arm and (to run) ____________ up the net curtains. It (to take) ____________ four neighbours half an hour to reach Tilly, who (to speed) ____________ up a tree. They (to fetch) ____________ a ladder, (to catch) ____________ Tilly and (to roll) ____________ her in a blanket, (to fasten) ____________ it with sticky tape and (to hand) ____________ her to Mrs Blake. She (to try) ____________ again. The neighbours (to hear) ____________ a shriek and (to run) ____________ into the house. Tilly (to hang) ____________ by her claws from the light. Three hours later Mr Blake (to appear) ____________ and (to ask) ____________ why his wife (to lie) ____________ on the sofa with both arms bandaged and why the poor little cat (to sit) ____________ on the roof.

Using verbs correctly

Objective

Use standard English forms for verbs.

Background knowledge

In standard English a verb should agree with its subject. Agreement in any tense is achieved using inflections, such as the irregular verb 'eat':

Singular present tense		
1st person	**2nd person**	**3rd person**
I eat	you eat	he/she/it eats
I am eating	you are eating	he/she/it is eating
Singular past tense		
I ate	you ate	he/she/it ate
I was eating	you were eating	he/she/it was eating

Plural present tense		
1st person	**2nd person**	**3rd person**
we eat	you eat	they eat
we are eating	you are eating	they are eating
Plural past tense		
we ate	you ate	they ate
we were eating	you were eating	they were eating

Activities

- **Photocopiable page 67 'Change the verb'**
The children will need to say the sentences aloud, sometimes saying them a few times as they rework them to natural language. There are various options for changing the sentences to make them sound right. Any variations can be compared and discussed as alternative ways of reworking the tense.

- **Photocopiable page 68 'Crazy verbs'**
These silly rhymes develop the children's awareness of the patterns for forming some irregular past tenses – and the odd ones out. They correct these so that they know the correct forms of the verbs, even though they are not nearly so much fun. If they find this difficult, ask them to look at the correct past tenses (such as 'sang'), identify their present tense ('sing') and describe how they changed. This may then help them to figure out the correct forms of the other verbs – although they are likely to need help with some, such as 'swang', which comes from 'swing' and should be 'swung'.

- **Photocopiable page 69 'Correct the sentences'**
Children identify verbs that are not in standard English and rewrite the sentences. Afterwards they could identify non-standard formations of verbs they use in informal speech or which they have heard others using.

Further ideas

- **I snoze, I blunk and I crew (I sneezed, I blinked and I cried):** Ask the children to make up silly sentences (perhaps arranging them in a rhyme) using invented forms of verbs based on the patterns of others. For example, the pattern 'sing'/'sang' could be applied to 'bring' to give 'brang'; 'grow'/'grew' suggests 'flow'/'flew'. They can then pass these to a partner who has to figure out what they mean and write the verbs correctly.
- **Past patterns:** Working in pairs, the children list verbs with the same present-tense endings as 'take', 'sing', 'weep', 'say', 'reach', 'sink', 'send', 'blow'. They group them according to past-tense patterns and notice any odd ones out. Challenge them to find others that match the odd ones. Note that 'sung' and 'rung' can only be used with an auxiliary verb such as 'has', 'have' or 'had' – similarly 'drink'/'drank'/'had drunk'.

Digital content

On the digital component you will find:

- Printable versions of all three photocopiable pages.
- Answers to all three photocopiable pages.
- Interactive versions of 'Change the verb' and 'Correct the sentences'.

Using verbs correctly

Change the verb

■ Correct the verb in each of these sentences. The first one has been done for you.

I found the shoe I lose. I found the shoe I lost.

Last week I see my aunty when she cycles to our house.

Yesterday we shall go to the shop and buy some new shoes.

When I went on the train I leave my umbrella.

Every time we do PE I jumped off the wall bars.

We started a game of football, then we stop when the bell ring.

We turn off the TV because there was nothing we wanted to watch.

I write a letter and then I posted it.

My brother wakes up late and rushed to school.

I tell my friend a joke yesterday.

Name:

Using verbs correctly

Crazy verbs

- Read the silly rhymes with a partner.
- Highlight any past tenses that are incorrect.
- See if you can figure out what verbs they are.
- Write the correct word in the margin.

The monkey sang as he swang in the tree
And threw a banana at me.

The sun shone, the wind blew and the grass grew,
but then it snew.
As the ship sank
We drank
Our tea and I thank
We would drown at sea.

Mr Grammaticus said, "I thought
That those were the books I bought."
But he put on his glasses and blought
His eyes.
His head shook and his hand quook
as he took the book.

Mr Spode strode down the road
But he slode on the ice and glode down the road.
Next time he rode.

Name:

Using verbs correctly

Correct the sentences

- Highlight any verbs that are not in standard English.
- Rewrite the sentences in standard English.

Dan were late as usual. His excuse was that he forgetting his homework.

I be good at maths and you be better at English. We both be good at football.

We taken a short cut but gotten lost.

He winded the clockwork toy but then losed the key.

We freezed the orange juice to make lollies. Soon they was solid.

The man tret the dog cruelly. It bitten him but he jumped in his car and drive away.

Nouns and determiners

Objective

Begin to understand the function of determiners and how they are used in writing.

Background knowledge

This section reminds children of the job a noun does in a sentence. A noun (or a pronoun, which represents a noun, for example, 'I', 'you', 'he', 'she', 'it', 'they') can be the subject of a verb in a sentence. Nouns that are not proper nouns (proper nouns are names of people, places, and so on, which begin with a capital letter) can be preceded by 'the', 'a' or 'an' – these words are, respectively, the definite article and the two forms of the indefinite article. The definite and indefinite articles are types of 'determiner' – words that specify a noun as known or unknown.

The activities in this section, along with the poster on page 57, help children to learn how determiners work in sentences. Other determiners include demonstratives (such as 'this', 'those', 'that'), possessives (such as 'my', 'his', 'your') and quantifiers (such as 'some', 'each', 'every'). A determiner always precedes the noun it refers to, and precedes any word that modifies the noun (such as adjectives or other nouns).

Activities

- **Photocopiable page 71 'A noun test'**

This page helps to consolidate previous learning about nouns by presenting nouns as words that can be introduced with the word 'the'. It is useful first to ask the children for some examples of nouns and to point out that nouns are not only words for objects but can be words for things we can't see, hear or touch, such as 'thought', 'feeling', 'idea'. These words make sense when 'the' is put in front of them. The children could suggest other words like this and then test whether they are nouns by adding 'the'. Note that 'noun' refers to how a word acts in a sentence; words such as 'walk', 'run' and 'treat' can act as a noun or a verb.

- **Photocopiable page 72 'Determiners'**

In this activity the children use the determiners 'the', 'a', 'an' or 'some' to introduce nouns. Ask them to try changing 'the' to 'a', 'an' or 'some' in sentences and to describe how this changes the meaning, for example: *We watched the sunset; The teacher asked the class to listen; This is the tree the owl was in; Look at the screen; Let's set up the goal posts; Can you reach the ceiling?* Note that plural abstract and mass nouns can make sense without any determiner, for example: *Pigs can't fly; Cities are bigger than towns; Silence is golden.*

- **Photocopiable page 73 'More determiners'**

In this activity the children use the determiners 'this', 'that', 'these' and 'those'. To explain the difference between 'this' and 'that', and 'these' and 'those', it is helpful to use objects that are positioned nearby and farther off and point to them using phrases such as *these chairs/those chairs, this table/that table.*

Further ideas

- **The titles:** Children could make notes of book titles or television programmes that contain 'a', 'an', 'the' or 'some', and try changing these, deciding whether it makes any difference to their meanings and, if so, what difference.
- **Some changes:** Introduce other determiners with different shades of meaning but similar to the word 'some', such as 'several', 'a lot of', 'many', 'few', 'a few', 'numerous' and 'any'. Ask children to write different versions of a sentence, substituting these words for 'some'. Discuss the subsequent changes to the meaning of the sentence.
- **This or that?:** Revise plurals before practising the use of 'this', 'that', 'these', 'those'. Also remind children about verb agreement ('this is' changes to 'these are', and so on).

Digital content

On the digital component you will find:

- Printable versions of all three photocopiable pages.
- Answers to all three photocopiable pages.
- Interactive versions of 'A noun test' and 'Determiners'.

Nouns and determiners

A noun test

If a word is a noun it makes sense when you put 'the' before it, unless it is a proper noun (the name of a person, place, book and so on).

■ Try writing 'the' before these words to decide whether they could be nouns.

Then tick the nouns. 

Some words could be nouns or other kinds of words, for example: walk (I **walk** every day. I'm going for **a walk**. Joe can **run** fast. He went for **a run**.)

_____ cheese ☐	_____ cry ☐	_____ sing ☐
_____ where ☐	_____ bread ☐	_____ butter ☐
_____ up ☐	_____ red ☐	_____ car ☐
_____ room ☐	_____ big ☐	_____ quickly ☐
_____ here ☐	_____ write ☐	_____ walk ☐
_____ carry ☐	_____ choose ☐	_____ clear ☐
_____ under ☐	_____ cat ☐	_____ answer ☐
_____ question ☐	_____ sorry ☐	_____ beginning ☐
_____ sand ☐	_____ size ☐	_____ idea ☐
_____ description ☐	_____ colourful ☐	_____ silly ☐
_____ understand ☐	_____ open ☐	_____ opening ☐

Name:

Nouns and determiners

Determiners

When you write 'the' before a noun this shows that is a particular thing, not just any thing. For example, *the dog* means a particular dog.

When you write *a dog*, this shows that you are talking about the dog for the first time. The plural of this is *some dogs*.

Words like 'the', 'a', 'an' or 'some' are used with nouns. They are called 'determiners'. They always come before the noun.

■ Write a determiner in each gap. Then underline the nouns.

Jenny's mum asked her to take ________ dog for a walk.

All ________ houses in our road have a tree in their garden.

There is ________ good film on television tonight.

I wonder if there is ________ orange in the fruit bowl.

Let's go and buy ________ sweets.

Most fairy tales begin 'Once upon ________ time'.

Harry asked me what ________ time was.

I'm going for ________ walk.

Pass me ________ salt, please.

We went out of our house and crossed ________ road.

Martina was very thirsty and hoped there was ________ apple juice in ________ fridge.

Mrs Parker was looking for ________ little cottage in ________ countryside.

She hoped she would find ________ old one with ________ thatched roof and ________ trees in the garden.

More determiners

Here are some useful determiners to use with nouns:

Singular	Plural	Singular	Plural
this	these	that	those

■ Rewrite each sentence, making the bold words plural.

This pencil is mine.

____________________ are mine.

Look at **this picture**.

That girl won two races on Saturday.

That turnip is enormous.

This biscuit is fresh but **that cake** is stale.

My dad made **this cake** and this sandwich, too, but my mum made **that pie**.

"Who let **that goat** into the garden?" shouted Mrs Roper.

I think **this book**, **this pen** and **that pencil** over there are mine.

Writing with accuracy

Objective

Use verbs, nouns and determiners consistently and accurately in writing.

Writing focus

Building on previous activities, this section encourages children to think consciously about their use of grammar in order to improve their writing.

Skills to writing

- **Verbs in stories**

Verbs are a great means of translating children's enjoyment of their reading into more imaginative writing. Take a look at the illustrations in favourite picture books and cover the text. Ask the children to come up with verbs for the actions in the pictures. This can provide an interesting way of summarising the key events of a story. Ask questions such as *Which five verbs could retell the story of Cinderella?*

- **Collections**

Make a collection of verbs for children to consider when writing. Encourage them to add to the collection as they come across other interesting verbs. Particular focus could be placed on words for movement ('ran', 'dashed', 'sauntered') and speech ('yelled', 'whispered', 'murmured') as these will prove to be a good resource in narrative writing. Other good collections can include words for seeking, finding, understanding and seeing.

- **Verb hunts**

This activity is linked to the one above. Children could look for new and interesting verbs in their reading. They might not be sure of the meaning but can figure this out from the context. This can be turned into a challenge – such as covering a 100-square wallchart with sticky notes and building up a collection of 'This month's 100 best verbs'. Every so often you could challenge children to make up a sentence using one of these verbs.

- **Focused revision**

Focus on a grammatical rule, such as pluralisation. Children can check their own writing for instances where they have deployed, or should have deployed, the rules for making pluralisation changes, especially where these involve verb agreement or changes to determiners.

- **Noun hunt**

On the whiteboard, display sections of text (fiction or non-fiction) that contain plenty of nouns accompanied by determiners and other words, such as *a gnarled old tree; some little green people; this brave young prince.* Ask the children to identify the nouns and then any determiners that come before them. Point out that other words that add to the meaning of the noun always follow the determiner.

Activities

- **Photocopiable page 76 'Story thinking'**

This set of phrases can be used as story-writing stimulus. The words can form a starting point for story writing or could be used by children who are planning a story to provide ideas of initial phrases they could use to generate some interesting sentences. Each phrase should engender some thought about what a character is thinking or feeling. Use this activity to help children to understand that verbs are not only words for actions but can also refer to thoughts, feelings, ideas and so on. The children can keep the examples in this activity in reserve for later use, or gather new examples from other verbs. Note that the 'she/he' alternatives present children with the chance to choose a character's gender.

- **Photocopiable page 77 'My verbs'**

This activity focuses on verbs children have used in their writing and draws attention to the verbs' tenses and how these are formed. This is designed to be a quick activity, securing the children's knowledge of the formation and use of tenses of verbs they have already used, with the possibility of exploring synonymous verbs. The starting point will depend on the verb form already used. The example begins with the past tense 'ran'; another tense that could have been used is the present tense 'run'. There is an explanation of how the verb changes to form these two tenses. Other verbs that could have been used should be, as here, words that are appropriate for the context.

Write on

- **Unusual instructions**

Ask children to write an instructional booklet on an imaginative topic such as 'Using a magic broomstick'; a guide for new secret agents, 'Using your gadgets' or a guide for aliens visiting Earth on how to use any familiar device.

- **Create verb-o-saurus posters**

Ask the children to devise posters for common verbs they will use in their writing, gathering new examples and writing examples of their use. If they have gathered these from a text, ask them to quote the source.

- **Unusual verbs**

Together, gather verbs that are commonly associated with one topic that can be applied to another. A useful consideration is to think of the image conjured up when certain unusual verbs are applied to a person. 'Slithered' is a verb that conjures up a reptilian image, so what image does this conjure up when it is applied to a teacher 'slithering' into the classroom? What about a child 'bouncing' down the corridor or someone 'dripping' down the corridor? This sort of innovative experiment can make for some interesting word usage. A very funny poem that matches verbs to teacher's names is 'At the End of School' by Simon Pitt.

- **The best determiners**

In non-fiction writing, particularly reports, focus on the determiners used with nouns. Sometimes words such as 'several', 'few' or 'numerous' can be more effective in communicating information than 'some'. Children could read through their reports and change one or two determiners where appropriate.

- **Determiner challenge**

Challenge children to write sentences using the determiners they have practised or – to increase the level of demand – using some of the less common determiners, such as 'any', 'each', 'every'. They should check that each determiner they use accompanies a noun and that it precedes the noun, but they could add other words, which should follow the determiner but precede the noun.

Digital content

On the digital component you will find:

- Printable versions of both photocopiable pages.

Name:

Writing with accuracy

Story thinking

- Think of story ideas built around these phrases.

Realising I was not alone...	Losing friends...
Breaking a promise...	Thinking of running away...
Discovering the truth...	Seeing her/him for the first time...
Understanding why she/he did it...	Knowing what was really going on...

Name:

Writing with accuracy

My verbs

■ Use this chart to analyse verbs you have used in your writing. An example has been completed to demonstrate how to do this.

The verb in my writing and the sentence I used it in	The tense I used	How to form this tense	Another tense of the verb	Other verbs I could have used
We ran back home.	Past	Change 'run' to 'ran' by changing the 'u' to 'a'	Present: We are running	dashed, raced

Chapter 4

Developing sentences

Introduction

This chapter helps children to create longer sentences that make use of expanded noun phrases and adverbials. They learn to consider the effects of different sentence lengths and where longer sentences are appropriate, understanding that sometimes a shorter sentence is better than a long one. For further practice, please see the 'Developing sentences' section of the Year 4 workbook.

Poster notes

Adding to a noun (page 79)
This explains noun phrases using the example of an alien whose appearance and demeanour become clearer to the observer as he/she/it approaches. As the alien approaches, more description is given through adding adjectives and adjectival phrases before or after the noun, as appropriate.

Adding to a verb (page 80)
This poster explains adverbials and shows how they can be added to a verb to say more about it. It helps to show that a sentence makes sense without the adverbial, but that it has less information.

In this chapter

Vocabulary

Children should already know:
noun, noun phrase, adverb, adjective

In Year 4 children need to know:
determiner, adverbial

Developing sentences

ADDING TO A NOUN

A noun phrase acts like a noun. It contains a noun, as well as other words that give information about the noun.
This noun is the main word in the phrase.
You can add words to a noun to make a **noun phrase**. You can add more words to the **noun phrase**.

An alien came down the road.

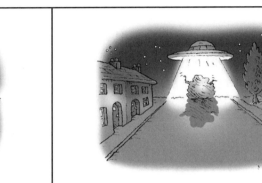

A large alien came down the road.

A large, green alien came down the road.

A large, green alien with three eyes came down the road.

A large, green alien with three eyes and a smiling face came down the road.

A large, green alien with three brown eyes and a smiling face came down the road.

Developing sentences

Adding to verb

An adverbial acts like an adverb. It is a phrase that gives information about a verb.
Some details that an adverbial can tell us are…

How something happens	Where something happens	When something happens
He walked **in a slow, careful way.**	He walked **along the wall.**	He raised his head **when he heard me.**
He walked **as if he had all day.**	He walked **through the gate.**	He raised his head **as the birds flew past.**
He walked **with long, slow steps.**	He walked **across the middle of the lawn.**	He raised his head **before climbing the wall.**
He walked **like a tortoise.**	**He walked around the edge of the pool.**	He raised his head **after the rain stopped.**

An adverbial can come before the verb:

How something happens	Where something happens	When something happens
In a flash, the thief disappeared.	**Along the path** was a trail of sweets.	**On Saturday** we went to the cinema.
With long slow steps, he climbed the hill.	**Down the road** came a noisy crowd.	**Before climbing the wall** he raised his head.
With his heart beating fast, he opened the door.	**All around him** were twinkling lights.	**At midnight** the clock began to chime.
In her sly way, she lied to me.	**Behind the cupboard** there were about a hundred spiders.	**That day** we knew we would win the competition.

Noun phrases

Objective

Consider how noun phrases can be expanded.

Background knowledge

This section introduces ways of expanding noun phrases by adding modifying adjectives, nouns and preposition phrases. It is useful to remind children about the job done by nouns in a sentence (they are the names of things, people, places and so on).

A noun phrase is a phrase headed by a noun (the noun is the most important word in the phrase, which could not stand without it). A noun phrase can be expanded by adding words such as an article, adjectives (and adjectival phrases), prepositions (and prepositional phrases) before or after the noun as appropriate. Importantly, a noun phrase acts as a noun in a sentence. For example, *The fox jumps over the dog* contains two nouns, 'fox' and 'dog', which can be made into noun phrases by adding adjectives: *The quick, brown fox jumps over the lazy dog*. The noun phrases could be expanded: ***The quick, brown fox with a large bushy tail*** *jumps over* ***the large, lazy dog that hardly ever moves***. Although there is a verb in the second noun phrase, the verb forms part of the noun phrase and modifies the noun.

Activities

- **Photocopiable page 82 'Build a noun phrase'**
In this activity the children add words to nouns to create noun phrases. As they do so, encourage them to consider how they can create different effects by changing these.
- **Photocopiable page 83 'Grow a noun phrase'**
This activity reminds children what a noun phrase is and, through using the idea of a pyramid, shows how it can be expanded by adding words. It is important to point out that the additions to the noun phrase that give extra information can consist of more than one word, for example: *in a desert, built by the Egyptians, thousands of years ago*.
- **Photocopiable page 84 'Expand it'**
In this activity the children identify places around a noun where they can add information to create an expanded noun phrase. Having identified these places they proceed to expand the noun phrases.

Further ideas

- **Shrink it:** Children could look at a range of texts to try and identify where a noun phrase has been 'expanded', which words have been added and how these change the noun. This could involve stripping the noun phrase back to the noun and commenting on the difference this makes.
- **Special effects:** Using different texts, children could identify nouns that are part of a noun phrase, and the words that form the noun phrase and add information to the noun. They could substitute these for others to create a different effect. Passages from Dickens novels could be useful for this.
- **Extra detail:** Provide passages from non-fiction texts that make use of noun phrases for adding information, for example: clothing and holiday brochures (printed or online), instructions, rules and regulations and estate agents' leaflets. Children could identify noun clauses and explain how they are useful and what they add.

Digital content

On the digital component you will find:

- Printable versions of all three photocopiable pages.
- Answers to 'Grow a noun phrase'.

Name:

Noun phrases

Build a noun phrase

■ Each picture has a caption that includes a noun. Write a word in the space to say what the object is like. This makes the caption a noun phrase.

the __________ hand	the __________ monster	the __________ spaceship
the __________ diary	the __________ star	the __________ cat
the __________ ring	the __________ dog	the __________ fire
the __________ mug	the __________ house	the __________ ball
the __________ pirate	the __________ bath	the __________ bird
the __________ snake	the __________ mouse	the __________ music
the __________ baby	the __________ dress	the __________ elephant

Noun phrases

Grow a noun phrase

When you expand something you make it bigger. You can add words to a noun phrase to expand it.

■ Add words to the noun phrase below to expand it. You can add these before or after the noun.

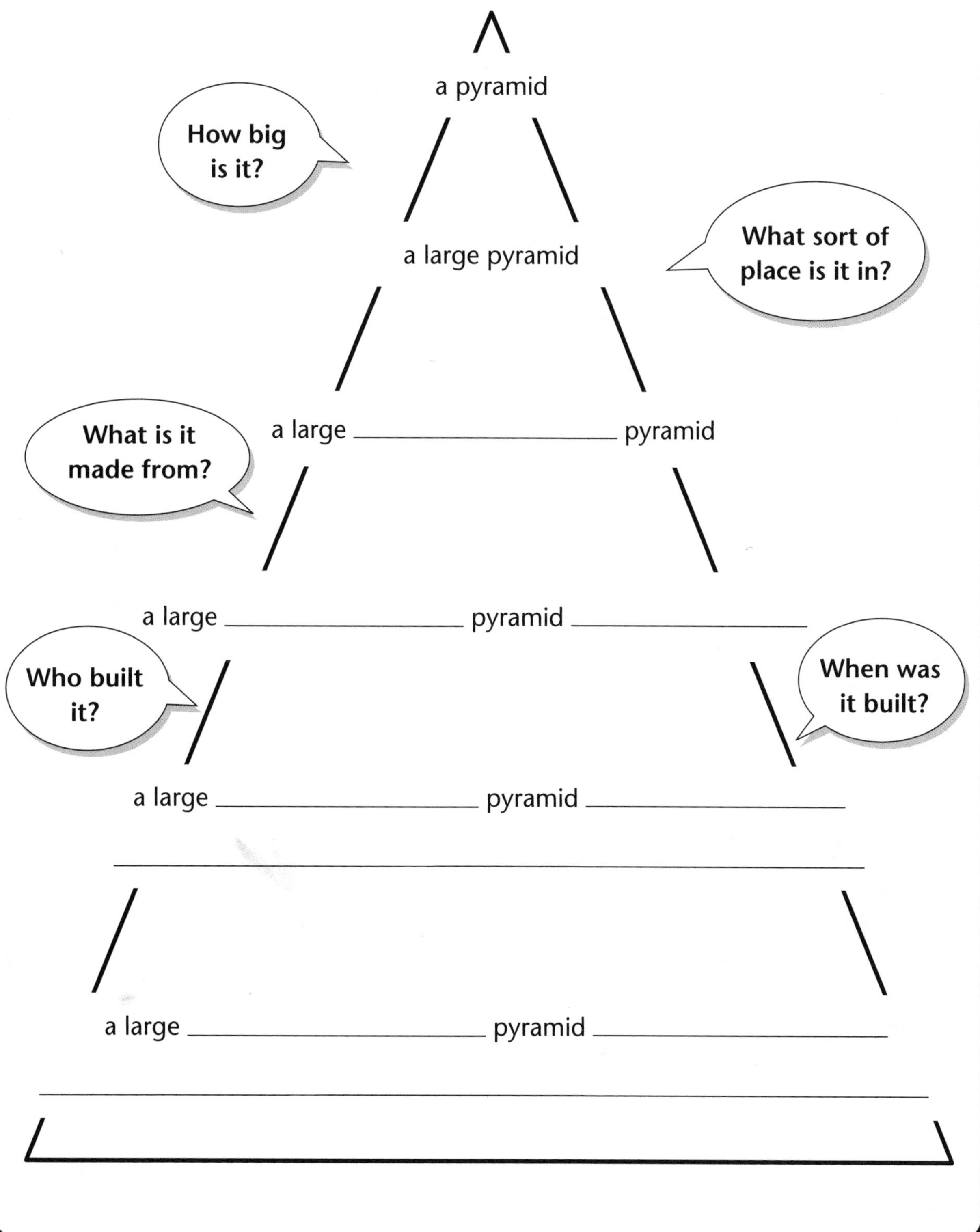

Name:

Noun phrases

Expand it

- Draw arrows to the spaces where you could add words.
- Add words to the nouns in each sentence to make noun phrases. The first one has been done for you.

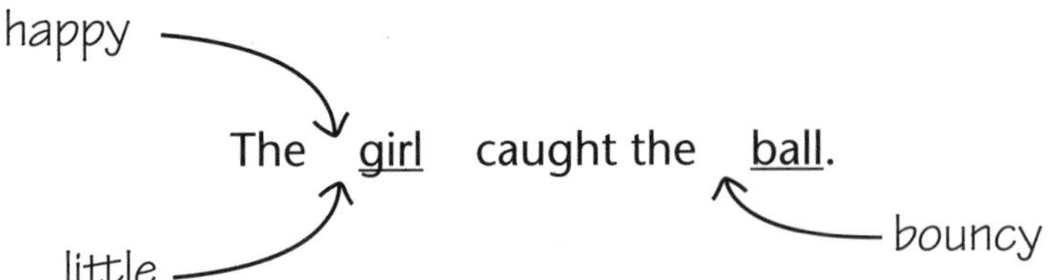

The bear hid behind a tree.

The boat crossed the river.

The wolf chased the duck.

The boy went on the bus to the shop.

My friend lives in a house in my street.

On the table at the party there was a cake.

The goblin lived in a den under the bridge.

The spaceship landed on the planet.

Expanding noun phrases

Objective

Expand noun phrases in writing.

Background knowledge

Building on the previous section, this section is about giving children opportunities to look at expanded noun phrases and to try using some of their own in their writing.

Activities

- **Photocopiable page 86 'Powerful noun phrases'**
This page provides a description with expanded noun phrases in bold. The children change any words except the nouns themselves to create a very different impression, for instance, they could describe a scruffy car and driver and make her unfriendly instead of friendly.
- **Photocopiable page 87 'Writing with noun phrases'**
Here the children are presented with a description that could be enhanced by expanding the noun phrases. They come up with their own words to add to the noun phrases, before or after the noun as appropriate. It is useful to remind them that they can add phrases to a noun phrase, for example: *her own home-made jam, her old, beaten-up jeep with rusty bumpers.*
- **Photocopiable page 88 'Noun phrases in my writing'**
This page provides a planning chart to help children to come up with useful noun phrases to use in a description of a place. This could be linked with work in geography on developing a sense of place.

Further ideas

- **Noun phrases in instructions:** Children could expand noun phrases to clarify instructions, for example, directions:
  - *Turn left after **the shop**.*
  - *Turn left after **the grocery shop**.*
  - *Turn left after **the grocery shop with the tables outside it**.*
  - *It is **the house at the end of the road**.*
  - *It is **the white house at the end of the road**.*
  - *It is **the small white house at the end of the first road on the right**.*
- **Noun phrases to answer questions:** Children ask questions that prompt the expansion of noun phrases. For example: *I saw the cat.*
Which cat?
I saw the black cat.
Which black cat?
I saw the black cat that lives at number 10.
- **Find your own noun phrases:** Children could read through some of their own writing and identify any noun phrases they have used. They could also find examples where they could improve their writing by expanding their noun phrases.

Digital content

On the digital component you will find:
- Printable versions of all three photocopiable pages.

Name:

Expanding noun phrases

Powerful noun phrases

- Rewrite this description, changing the noun phrases in bold to give a different impression of the car and its driver.
- Don't change the nouns, just the other words in the noun phrases.
- Add extra words to these phrases if you wish.

A shiny red sports car came down the hill. **A purring noise** came from the engine as it passed. Then it stopped and **a smart young woman** wearing **a crisp white blouse** and **designer jeans** opened **the gleaming door** and stepped out and gave **a friendly wave** to the children who gathered around to look at **the amazing car**.

"Look at **those thick, new tyres**!" said one. Another pointed out **the soft, comfortable leather seats**. A third said she had never seen such **a clean, shiny car**.

Name:

Writing with noun phrases

Leo wrote this description of his grandmother.

- Rewrite it, expanding the noun phrases in bold to create an impression of Leo's grandmother.
- Remember that you can add words before or after the noun – or both.

My grandmother lives in **a cottage**. In **her front garden** there are **flowers**. In **her back garden** there are **vegetables and fruit**. She has **a field behind the house** where she has **henhouses** for **her hens**.

Twice a week she drives into town in **her jeep** to sell **eggs, vegetables and fruit** to **restaurants**. She also sells **jam** at **the farmers' market**.

Gran hardly buys any food at **the shops**. She even goes to **the river** to fish.

Name:

Expanding noun phrases

Noun phrases in my writing

- Use this page to plan a short description of a place you know.
- Think about how you can use noun phrases to tell a reader what the place is like.

Place:	
Type of place	Useful noun phrases
Where it is	Useful noun phrases
What it is like	Useful noun phrases
Special things to see	Useful noun phrases

What is an adverbial?

Objective

Understand what an adverbial is and identify adverbials in texts.

Background knowledge

An adverbial is a word or phrase that modifies a verb or clause – it says something about the verb or the entire clause the verb is in, for example:

- *He ran **like the wind**.* (Says how he ran.)
- *We're going on holiday **next week**.* (Says when we are going on holiday. This adverbial modifies the clause *We're going on holiday*.)

Sometimes the adverbial is moved so that it precedes the verb instead of following it. This is known as a 'fronted adverbial', for example:

- ***Next week** we're going on holiday.* (Instead of *We're going on holiday **next week**.*)
- ***After finishing her homework**, Emma went to bed.* (Instead of *Emma went to bed **after finishing her homework**.*)
- In most cases it is necessary to insert a comma after a fronted adverbial: ***Before we leave**, let's check that we've turned everything off.* This use of a comma is covered in more detail in Chapter 6 (Punctuation).

Although children should be introduced to the term 'adverbial', they do not necessarily need to know the term 'fronted adverbial' – just that the adverbial can come before the verb or clause.

Activities

- **Photocopiable page 90 'How verbs happen'**
Through considering the phrases that say more about the verbs in the sentences, the children should begin to understand what an adverbial does. To introduce adverbials, the focus here is on what they say about how, where or when the verb happens. Stress to the children that they are looking for words or phrases that say something about the verb and could be removed from the sentence without changing the sense.
- **Photocopiable page 91 'Adverbial purposes'**
Three broad purposes of adverbial are presented: how, where and when. Encourage the children to look at the adverbial as an answer to a question about the action. What question could it be answering? Does the adverbial answer how, when or where?
- **Photocopiable page 92 'Adverbials in action'**
The children read a passage, identify the verbs and, as they do so, check for an adverbial that says more about the verb (How? When? Where?). Tell them that this could come before or after the verb. The completed example shows a fronted adverbial (an adverbial that precedes the verb): *The previous day they had seen....*

Further ideas

- **How do you do that?:** Children devise questions that are answerable using adverbials, such as *How do you walk into a classroom when you are late?* or *How do you walk past a snarling dog?* They can put these to one another and note any adverbials used to answer each question.
- **Adverbial of the day:** Children collect examples of interesting adverbials from printed or online texts. They choose the one they think is the most imaginative to present to the class, then vote for the 'adverbial of the day (or week)'.
- **More than one adverbial:** Using passages chosen from books, children look for verbs that are modified by more than one adverbial. Can they find any examples of three or more adverbials for one verb? The challenge could be to find the verb that has the most adverbials.

Digital content

On the digital component you will find:

- Printable versions of all three photocopiable pages.
- Answers to all three photocopiable pages.
- Interactive version of 'How verbs happen' and 'Adverbial purposes'.

Name:

What is an adverbial?

How verbs happen

■ Look at each of these examples and find the verbs (the actions or happenings) and the words that tell us about the verb. The first one has been done for you.

The boy quickly ran downstairs.		We played well on the muddy field.	
Verb	**Words about the verb**	**Verb**	**Words about the verb**
ran	quickly, downstairs		
Turn the bottle top until it clicks.		I planted the seeds in the garden.	
Verb	**Words about the verb**	**Verb**	**Words about the verb**
We will sing sweetly at the wedding today.		Listen as carefully as you can to the message.	
Verb	**Words about the verb**	**Verb**	**Words about the verb**

What is an adverbial?

Adverbial purposes

Adverbials say something about a verb, such as how it happened:

He ran **like the wind**.

Adverbials tell us where it happened:

He ran **all the way upstairs**.

They tell us when it happened:

Later that day, he ran a race.

how
where
when

- Underline the adverbials in these sentences.
- Decide what the adverbials tell us about the verbs.
- Write how, when or where on the line.

Adverb describes:

Ellie sang like a lark. how

Let's go to the park after school. ________

In the summer holidays there is no school. ________

Put the chair beside the table. ________

He slipped into the pond. ________

I will text you on Saturday morning. ________

Speed cameras appeared on each main road. ________

The burglar tiptoed past the guard dog. ________

The sun rose at five o'clock. ________

We saw no stars in the sky. ________

Our cat barks like a dog. ________

The crane pulled the car out of the mud. ________

The pirate buried the treasure near the cave. ________

We said "Goodbye" with heavy hearts. ________

I am going swimming in the new pool. ________

Name:

What is an adverbial?

Adverbials in action

■ Read the introduction to *It's Too Frightening for Me!* by Shirley Hughes:

Jim and Arthur lived near an eerie house. The previous day they had seen a strange girl's face at a window.

Next day they watched from the wall for a long time, but no face appeared. Then Jim noticed a basement door at the bottom of a flight of steps, where the shutter had slipped and a glass pane was broken.

Jim slithered down into the yard and tried the door. It opened! Putting his finger to his lips, Jim made signs to Arthur to stay where he was. Then he disappeared into the house.

Poor Arthur! He badly wanted to run home, but he couldn't desert his brother. After a long while, he too climbed softly down into the yard and, trembling all over, crept in through the basement door to look for Jim.

■ Some of the verbs from the story are listed. Find them in the passage then look for adverbials that say more about them. (There might be more than one.) The first has been done for you.

Verb	**Adverbials**	**What it tells us about the verb**
had seen	the previous day	When they saw the face
lived		
watched		
slithered		
stay		
disappeared		
climbed		
crept		

Using adverbials

Objective

Begin to use adverbials in writing.

Background knowledge

Children will have learned that an adverbial is a word or phrase that modifies a verb or clause – it says something about the verb or the entire clause containing the verb. They will know that adverbials sometimes come before the verb. They could begin to use commas, where necessary, when they use an adverbial before the verb, but this will be covered in more detail in Chapter 6 (Punctuation).

Activities

- **Photocopiable page 94 'Adverbial links'**
This is an investigative activity in which groups of three children explore the type of action and sentence they associate with a particular adverbial. The emphasis is on the collation of their findings and any patterns they find when they cut out their sentences, group those together with the same adverbials and glue them onto a large sheet. They should notice that the adverbials in this activity say how the verb was carried out.
- **Photocopiable page 95 'Tell us more'**
This activity gives children an opportunity to experiment with their own production of adverbials. They could use a list of adverbials compiled by the whole class.
- **Photocopiable page 96 'Adverbials at the front'**
In this activity the children add adverbials to sentences, positioning them before the verb and adding a comma after the adverbial, if they think it is necessary for clarity. You may wish to provide extra paper for children to write longer sentences.

Further ideas

- **Comic pages:** Provide the children with comics and ask them to make a list of the pictorial representations of actions that they can see on the pages. They can then use adverbials to describe the manner in which each action is being done.
- **Modify it:** Invite the children to produce simple sentences that include the words 'Albert collapsed'. They think of words to add to their starter clause (for example: *Albert collapsed in a heap in the gutter*), gradually producing a lengthy sentence with more than one adverbial modifying the verb. Remind them that an adverbial can come before the verb and might need a comma after it.
- **Collecting adverbs:** As with many of the types of words looked at in this book, an enriching follow-up activity involves children collecting examples. Invite the children to make a list of new and interesting adverbial words and phrases as they read various texts.

Digital content

On the digital component you will find:

- Printable versions of all three photocopiable pages.

Name:

Using adverbials

Adverbial links

- On a separate sheet of paper, write a sentence using each adverbial below. Don't look at anyone else's in your group!
- Compare your sentences. Do you notice any similarities?
- Write what you found out.

Adverbial	What we found out
at the top of his voice	
as if it were his favourite food	
in hushed voices	
at the last minute	
with slow steady strides	
with tears in her eyes	
without stopping to think	
with his heart beating fast	

Using adverbials

Tell us more

A sentence could say:

Lucy fell.

If we add an adverbial it could say:

At that moment Lucy fell off her chair with a loud crash.

■ In the boxes below, draw pictures of people (or animals or monsters!) doing things. In the box below each drawing, write a sentence saying what is happening. Use an adverbial to give details of what is happening. The first one has been done for you.

Picture	Picture	Picture
Sentence Daniel wrote his story at lightning speed.	Sentence	Sentence
Picture	Picture	Picture
Sentence	Sentence	Sentence

Name:

Using adverbials

Adverbials at the front

- Look for the verb in each sentence.
- Rewrite the sentence with an adverbial that makes sense in front of the verb, for example:

I lose my keys.
Every morning I lose my keys.

Sometimes you will need a comma after the adverbial, for example: *In the meantime, please pass me that book.*

I take my umbrella with me.

____

I give my dog a treat.

____

There's no point in asking Dad to help.

____

The search-and-rescue team climbed the cliff.

____

I couldn't find anything for Mum's birthday.

____

Helen spotted Sarah and Mariam.

____

We picked up three bags of logs.

____

My brother and sister won a quiz.

____

Developing sentences

Objective

Develop sentences by using expanded noun phrases and adverbials in writing.

Writing focus

Building on previous activities, this section offers children opportunities to add information to their sentences through the use of expanded noun phrases and adverbials.

Skills to writing

- **Noun phrase rebounds**

Words added to noun phrases to expand them say more about nouns that could stand alone. To help children to develop their understanding of noun phrases it is important that they consider the ways in which they could use them in their own writing. To do this they can use 'noun phrase rebounds', in which they edit their own work, revisiting sentences they have written and considering ways to expand any noun phrases in them.

- **Story description**

In story writing, encourage children to develop one or two paragraphs that give the best description of the most important place or person in their text. If, for example, they are writing a story set in a fairy-tale palace, encourage them to spend time picturing and describing the palace, reminding them to use interesting noun phrases. Ask the children to pick apart and describe various aspects of the setting – again using effective noun phrases.

- **Poetic noun phrases**

Poetry writing provides a good resource for locating and collecting noun phrases used for their effect. The poem 'The Listeners', by Walter de la Mare, includes some atmospheric examples children can appreciate and use to improve their own writing. When it comes to writing, simply gathering and shaping expanded noun phrases related to a subject can result in poetic sentences. These can be put together to create a free verse.

- **Connections with nouns**

Grasping the use of noun phrases is a two-way process. It's not enough just to learn a collection of noun phrases or words to expand them – children need to consider how to create effective noun phrases. It helps if they say these aloud, thinking about the effects they create and, if the effect is not what they intend, changing some of the words.

- **Text types**

Notice which types of noun phrase appear in which types of text, for example: football reports, estate agents' information leaflets or online brochures, recipes and menus and other contexts, such as television programmes. Children can listen and look out for noun phrases in other contexts. For example, are certain noun phrases particular to dance contests, food advertisements, car programmes or mystery stories?

- **Characterisation**

Characterisation is the means whereby writers present their characters to the reader. Noun phrases play an obvious part in direct characterisation, where the narrator just says *He had a face that was lined like an old map* or *…with shoulders the width of a doorway…*. The more subtle type of characterisation is to influence the reader's view of a character by showing us what they looked like (*eyes sunk into deep sockets*) and placing them in a context (*in a classroom full of stuffed animals*). As they describe both appearance and context, children need to consider how these will affect the reader's perception of their character.

- **Inserts**

Look for opportunities to add words to a sentence. This is particularly relevant for expanding noun phrases and for adding adverbials. Children also need to develop an appreciation of when they have included enough – and not overdo the expansion of noun phrases or adverbials.

- **Adding information**

One way of developing sentence construction when working with non-fiction texts, is to review the opportunities to add information in sentences through the use of expanded noun phrases and adverbials. By using texts already in existence you can annotate them with questions about the subject. The next step is to come up with some answers and then to find ways of adding these into the text that is already there.

Activities

- **Photocopiable page 99 'Two different atmospheres'**

This provides a structure to help children to create two different atmospheres for old houses, using the same basic framework and expanding the noun phrases in different ways and adding different adverbials. For most children, it will be useful to help them to get started by asking them to say what kind of word has gaps around it. If it is a noun, they should create an expanded noun phrase around it; if it is a verb they should think of adverbials to add – as shown in the completed examples.

- **Photocopiable page 100 'For and against'**

In this activity children use noun phrases and adverbials to help them to express two opposing opinions. As in the previous activity, it helps if they first identify the types of word that the gaps could be linked to: for a noun they create an expanded noun phrase; for a verb they add an adverbial.

Write on

- **Fear**

Begin by reading passages from stories where tension or fear is built through the use of expanded noun phrases or adverbials. Children can identify these and point out the noun or verb. They can then create a scene in which a character faces something scary. It is probably easier to start with the nouns. Ask: *What would he/she see and hear?* Once they have planned these nouns, they need to reflect on the noun phrases they can build around them. One step in between is to ask the children to come up with questions that the noun phrases can answer. The next step is to consider the verbs they can use and then to ask questions that can be answered by adverbials.

- **Noun phrase collage**

Over time, cut out noun phrases from newspapers, adverts, posters and other texts. The children can use these to build up a collage. Ask them to glue any examples they find on a large sheet of paper, building up a collage from the centre outwards. It can stimulate some good discussion at home as to how the phrases affect the text.

- **Jabber**

Children can use 'Jabberwocky' by Lewis Carroll as the starting point for their own nonsense verses, in which they create noun phrases. It is not as easy as it first sounds, particularly if they want their text to sound like the feelings it is trying to evoke. The children will need an underlying narrative, such as someone losing and finding a treasure. Once the treasure is in its nonsense form, it will need an appropriate nonsense description.

- **Villains**

Villains are great fun to create. A good exercise on characterisation is to generate villains. Children can start by listing the top ten villains and identify any noun phrases or adverbials that made them appear villainous. How would they use noun phrases to describe the appearance of a Cruella de Vil or the Wicked Witch of the West? What about Dracula's castle? How did that enhance his character? What adverbials are used to create an sense of their actions? Having gathered examples, children can use these to stimulate the construction of, and language used for, their own example.

- **Adverbial mapping**

Children can use adverbials as a way of extending their planning and mapping out of narrative writing. As they plan a storyline they can consider how, where and when the various actions were done. This provides a useful way of engaging children with the emotions of the characters in their story. They will often envisage a basic action, such as *a scared boy escaping*. However, if they think of this as *a scared boy with his heart beating fast escaping into the woods*, they have started to work through the emotions that are featuring in their narrative.

Digital content

On the digital component you will find:

- Printable versions of both photocopiable pages.

Developing sentences

Two different atmospheres

■ Look at the titles of the two descriptions of old houses.

■ Complete the descriptions by adding noun phrases or adverbials to create two different effects, to match the titles. Some have been done for you as examples.

You don't need to fill every gap – just use the ones you need.

A charming old house

The lovely old house was built with care at the end of a sleepy country lane lined with flowers that perfume the air. ______ windows ______ ______ on either side of the ______ front door ______.

In the ______ garden was a ______ swing and ______ seesaw ______ among the ______.

I stepped ______ and looked ______ at what was behind it.

A creepy old house

The decrepit, crumbling old house was built in a dark, damp, hollow at the end of a dirt track full of litter. ______ windows ______ ______ on either side of the ______ front door ______.

In the ______ garden was a ______ swing and ______ seesaw ______ among the ______.

I stepped ______ and looked ______ at what was behind it.

Name:

Developing sentences

For and against

There is a plan to put wind turbines near the village. Some people are for this: they think it's a good idea. Others are against it.

- Complete the two reports: for and against wind turbines.
- Expand the noun phrases and add adverbials in the gaps.

Some have been done for you as examples.

You don't need to fill all the gaps.

For wind turbines

We welcome the wind turbines with open arms. They will produce clean electricity without pollution. They will send no ________ fumes ________ and our ________ streams will stay ________ for ________. The wind blows ________ and it's free, so we should use it ________. These ________ wind turbines standing ________ will be ________ attractive than ________ coal or gas power stations or ________ energy.

Against wind turbines

We are ________ against wind turbines. They will be a ________ blot on our ________ landscape. ________ will hear ________ noise as the blades turn ________ to produce ________ for ________. We live in a ________ place and will ________ oppose this ________ eyesore. ________ we will take a ________ petition to the Prime Minister ________.

Chapter 5

Cohesion

Introduction

This chapter focuses on cohesive devices: the words and phrases that help to link parts of a text, making links between and within paragraphs and between and within sentences. Pronouns and determiners are particularly useful for this, with pronouns sometimes acting as determiners, for example: ***This** is **the** place **where** we found **the** old chest*. For further practice, please see the 'Cohesion' section of the Year 4 workbook.

Poster notes

Hard-working pronouns (page 102)
The poster provides a useful reference for some of the jobs that pronouns can do. Children in Year 4 need to know the terms 'pronoun' and 'possessive pronoun' and some of their uses, including providing linkage between parts of a sentence or text.

Linking up (page 103)
This shows some of the devices that can be used to create cohesion within and between sentences and paragraphs. These words can also provide cohesion between larger units of text, such as chapters or entire books. The poster can be used as a reminder for children as they write, especially for longer texts, suggesting ways in which they can link parts of the text. For each example in the table it is useful to point out how the link word avoids repetition while linking ideas in the same or different sentences.

In this chapter

Vocabulary

Children should already know:
noun, noun phrase

In Year 4 children need to know:
determiner, pronoun, possessive pronoun

Cohesion

Hard-working pronouns

Replace nouns to avoid repetition

Rachel got up. Then Rachel had breakfast before brushing Rachel's hair.

Rachel got up. Then **she** had breakfast before brushing **her** hair.

Show possession

Rachel ate **her** breakfast.

I'll get **my** books.

The dog is **mine**.

Make links

I wrote to thank the boy **who** found my purse.

I went to see the house **that** Jack built.

Pronouns work hard.

Here are some of the things they do.

Link to something already mentioned in a sentence

She made the boat **herself**.

I made breakfast for **myself**.

Point something out

This is the house that Jack built.

That is the only way out.

Cohesion

Linking up

Some words and phrases are useful for making links between parts of a text.
They save you repeating things, for example:

"I went to watch Liverpool v Manchester United. ***The*** *match was Liverpool's first of the season."*

The before **match** says which match it was. It saves you repeating **Liverpool v Manchester United**.

Words	Example	What the words link with
they	I learned some French words on holiday. **They** were useful at the shops.	words
this	**This** was much more fun than just speaking English.	learning French words
that	**That** was my favourite holiday ever.	the holiday in the last two sentences
he	Dad didn't learn any French. **He** just spoke more loudly, but in English.	Dad
when	Mum said she'd test me on my French words **when** we got back.	Mum's test on French words
before, she, it	**Before** we went we had to take our dog to the vet for a rabies injection. **She** didn't seem to mind **it**.	to France, the dog, the rabies injection
too	She had to be microchipped, **too**.	the rabies injection
both	**Both** were expensive.	rabies injection and microchip

Nouns and pronouns

Objective

Revisit nouns and pronouns and their functions in sentences.

Background knowledge

In most sentences a noun is needed as the subject of verb. For example, in the sentence *The children went up the hill*, 'children' is the noun that is the subject of the verb 'went'. A noun that is not a proper noun can be preceded by 'the' (a few proper nouns, such as 'the Houses of Parliament' and 'the Parthenon' are preceded by 'the'). Nouns can be replaced by pronouns such as 'they', 'it', 'he', or 'she'. Sometimes it isn't clear which noun a pronoun refers to. For example, in *The dog jumped onto the wall just before it collapsed*, the pronoun 'it' could refer to the dog or the wall. To make the meaning clear, the word order of the sentence could be changed to *Just before the wall collapsed, the dog jumped onto it.*

Activities

- **Photocopiable page 105 'Find the pronouns'**

This activity acts as revision and involves children locating pronouns in sentences. Children could begin by deleting words they are sure are not pronouns. After completing this, children could also identify any nouns in the sentences.

- **Photocopiable page 106 'Two ways of reading it'**

The ambiguity of pronouns can result in some interesting sentences. In these examples there are two ways of reading each sentence. The children identify these and enjoy the humour of the incorrect one. Afterwards they could also explore ways of clarifying the meaning of each sentence, for example, changing the word order.

- **Photocopiable page 107 'The door'**

Here children are asked to locate the words that make links between parts of a sentence or between ideas in different sentences or paragraphs in a story. These are referred to as 'link words', rather than pronouns, because of their function: some are pronouns; others are not. Encourage pairs to discuss how the link words work and whether they think it is clear what the link words mean in each case.

Further ideas

- **Something else:** *Something Else* by Kathryn Cave (Puffins Books) is a picture book in which the characters' names are made up of pronouns. It proves to be an excellent story about how an 'I' accepts a 'You', making a 'They' friendship. Read it together, focusing on the pronouns.
- **Make it clear:** Provide humorous sentences from sources such as newspaper headlines or advertisements for the children to rewrite in sentence form, using pronouns to give greater clarity. You could find these in printed or online collections. A printed 'anthology' of these that is suitable for children is *The World's Stupidest Headlines* by Michael O'Mara (Michael O'Mara Books). Example sentences include *Hole appears in road, police looking into it.*

Digital content

On the digital component you will find:

- Printable versions of all three photocopiable pages.
- Answers to all three photocopiable pages.
- Interactive versions of 'Find the pronouns' and 'Two ways of reading it'.

Nouns and pronouns

Find the pronouns

■ Find the pronouns in these sentences and circle them.

This is my house.

That is the fire escape.

Here is the girl who lost her bike.

They tidied the bedroom.

She is playing football with him.

I can cook for myself.

This is the book that I lost yesterday.

My mum treated herself to this bar of chocolate.

Name:

Nouns and pronouns

Two ways of reading it

■ Each of these sentences could be read in two ways. In the first one the pronoun 'He' could mean the dog – or Harry! Try finding the possible double meanings for each sentence.

My friend Harry has got a dog. He is smelly.

Harry smells. The dog smells.

Our school had a bike shed but it got knocked down.

The teachers played football against the children and they lost.

My brother and sister found some broken toys so we put them in the bin.

Our teacher has got a gerbil. We like watching him run round in his wheel.

My sisters fed the rabbits. They have floppy ears and funny teeth.

Nouns and pronouns

The door

■ Circle the link words in this text. Add arrows to show what they link to. Two have been done for you.

The story with a creepy house

The children approached the house that stood, deserted, beyond some trees. They were all scared but Amrit persuaded them to walk right up to the open door that she had seen from the road. She pushed it.

"Where are you going?" somebody asked.

"I'm going in there," she replied "I am not going back."

Someone said "We won't go in there."

"Suit yourself," she said, too late.

They had run away.

She stepped inside, saying to herself, "I don't need them. I can look after myself," as the door creaked shut behind her.

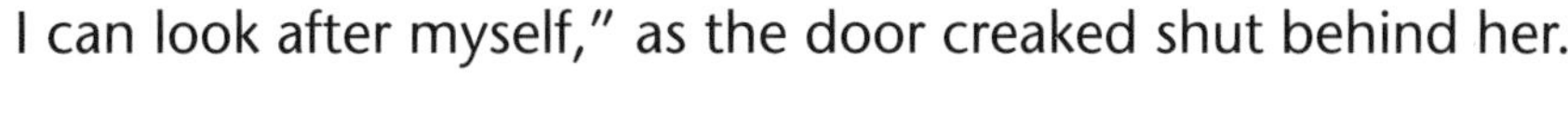

Choosing nouns and pronouns

Objective

Choose nouns and pronouns to aid clarity and cohesion and avoid repetition.

Background knowledge

Pronouns refer to nouns. They can show possession, for example: 'my'/'mine', 'your'/'yours', 'his', 'her'/'hers', 'its', 'our'/'ours', 'their'/'theirs' (see Chapter 2). They can replace a noun, acting as a determiner, for example: 'I'/'me', 'you', 'he'/'him', 'she'/'her', 'it', 'us'/'we', 'they'/'them', 'this', 'that' (see Chapter 3). They can be used to avoid repetition of a noun, but care needs to be taken to avoid confusion, for example: *The woman brought her dog. She was small with very long ears. Jack said they saw the sheep during their cycle ride, adding that they were wearing their safety helmets.*

In addition to their use in avoiding repetition, pronouns are useful in making links between sentences and paragraphs: *He cut the tree down because it was dangerous. It was a sycamore.*

The pronouns which begin with 'wh' are especially useful in this respect: *She bought a new car, which was much bigger than her old one. I met the girl who came to see us last week.*

Activities

- **Photocopiable page 109 'Pronoun or noun?'**
This provides a choice of pronouns or nouns from which children select the most appropriate for the sentence. It requires them to use pronouns, where appropriate, to avoid repetition, bearing in mind whether readers will know what the pronoun means (whether it refers to a noun that has been mentioned – linking parts of the text).

- **Photocopiable page 110 'Choose the right word'**
There are only certain words that will fit the spaces in these sentences. Children will need to read around the spaces, looking at other parts of the sentence that give clues as to which word should be used. They can also use a process of elimination, looking out for the words that do not fit and, on this basis, work out which words do.

- **Photocopiable page 111 'Too many pronouns'**
This helps children to understand how the clarity of sentences needs to be balanced against the avoidance of repetition. Encourage them to ask themselves questions such as those provided at the start. If the text doesn't provide the answer, they should check whether a pronoun needs to be replaced with a suitable noun. They have the opportunity to be inventive regarding the nouns they use.

Further ideas

- **Retell stories:** Children can try retelling well-known stories as pronoun tales, seeing how reductive their result can be and if anyone can recognise the original story from the end result. For example: *They went out. She came in. Didn't eat his. Didn't eat hers but did eat his. Didn't sit on his, didn't sit on hers but did sit on his....* Do you recognise 'Goldilocks and the Three Bears'?
- **Script pointing:** Look in playscripts to see how items and people in the text are referred to using pronouns and how this may lead the actor to point or use other gestures to indicate who is being referred to.
- **Seeing links:** In pairs, read familiar fiction or information books connected with work in other subjects, identifying words that make links within and between sentences, within and between paragraphs and even within and between chapters.

Digital content

On the digital component you will find:
- Printable versions of all three photocopiable pages.
- Answers to all three photocopiable pages.
- Interactive versions of 'Pronoun or noun?' and 'Choose the right word'.

Choosing nouns and pronouns

Pronoun or noun?

■ Underline a noun, noun phrase or pronoun from the brackets to fill each gap in this recipe.
■ Check that you don't repeat the nouns too often and that the meaning of each pronoun is clear.

Ice-cream ingredients: 300ml single cream, 1 teaspoon vanilla essence, 4 eggs, 300ml double cream, 100g sugar

1. Pour (**it** / **the single cream**) into a pan with (**it** / **the vanilla essence**) and heat until (**it** / **the single cream**) is just beginning to steam.

2. Take (**the pan** / **them** / **they**) off the heat and stir in the beaten eggs and sugar.

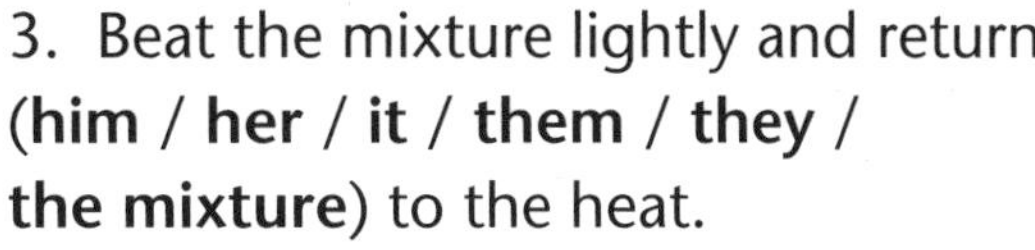

3. Beat the mixture lightly and return (**him** / **her** / **it** / **them** / **they** / **the mixture**) to the heat.

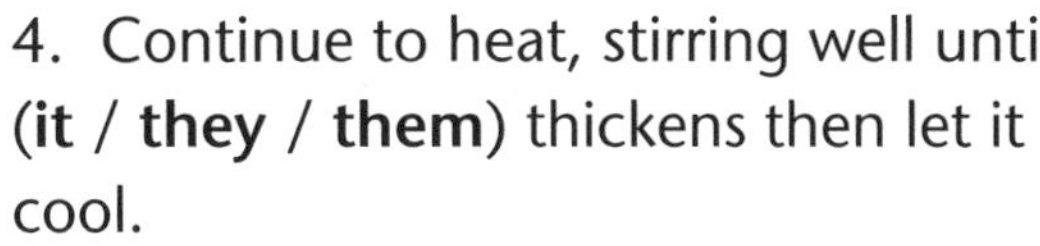

4. Continue to heat, stirring well until (**it** / **they** / **them**) thickens then let it cool.

5. Add (**it** / **the double cream** / **them** / **they**) to (**it** / **them** / **they** / **her** / **him** / **the mixture**) and stir well.

6. Pour (**it** / **the mixture**) into a bowl and put it in (**it** / **the freezer**).

7. Every hour, for three hours, take (**them** / **the mixture**) out and mix well with a fork.

Name:

Choosing nouns and pronouns

Choose the right word

- Write a noun (or nouns) or a pronoun in each gap.
- Check that the meaning of each pronoun is clear. If not, use a noun.

Yesterday ______________ were climbing a tree. Sara was climbing faster.

Roop was a bit slower but ______________ said, "______________ are the best climbers."

Sara waved ______________ arms and said, "Look at ______________ ______________ am better than ______________."

Roop said, "Don't say that. ______________ isn't a race."

Sara said, "Yes ______________ is and ______________ am winning."

Just then ______________ foot slipped. ______________ grabbed a branch.

"Careful! ______________ nearly fell," ______________ shouted.

______________ both started to climb down.

Roop I they me I

her her Sara

it she Roop and Sara

you we it Roop

Choosing nouns and pronouns

Too many pronouns

■ In this passage it isn't clear what some of the pronouns mean. Underline them and, above the pronouns, write nouns to replace them so that the news report makes sense.

■ You will need to read the whole passage before you can decide what nouns to write. The questions in the speech bubble will help you to get started.

Who? What did he break into?
What does he always wear?
What do they leave footprints in?

He was found guilty of breaking into it during the night. There had been several burglaries during that month and they think he is the culprit. He always wears them and they leave distinctive footprints in it. He always takes them and never bothers with them. Perhaps they are easier to sell. He was found trying to sell one in a local pub. They became suspicious and phoned them. They caught him red-handed and arrested him. He said someone gave it to him in exchange for it. However, they used a light to reveal their house number and postcode written on the back of it. They said they hadn't given it to him in exchange for it. Summing up, he said that he was a nuisance to them and sentenced him to three months in jail.

Using paragraphs in writing

Objective

Use paragraphs to organise ideas around a theme.

Background knowledge

A paragraph is a section of text organised around a topic. It is separated visually from any previous paragraph by its beginning on a new line, usually indented. The first sentence of the new paragraph very often says what the paragraph is about, for example:

Jason could never keep his written work tidy or clean. There would be fingerprints on it, mistakes crossed out all over the place and no line was ever straight. Even if he remembered to use a ruler, the ruler would slip and the line would veer off in an unintended direction.

The paragraph topic is Jason's untidiness – introduced in the first sentence, after which there is more information, with examples.

Activities

- **Photocopiable page 113 'Story paragraphs'**

Here the children summarise the action/main event of each paragraph in a story. They develop their understanding of how paragraphs can be useful in organising the events of a story. They could also look at how authors of stories they know have split the action into separate paragraphs.

- **Photocopiable page 114 'Paragraph topics'**

In this activity the children read a descriptive passage about a character. Each paragraph here presents information about the character and builds up a picture of him. The children learn how paragraphs can be used for organising text into topics as they identify the topic of each paragraph. Encourage them to underline any key sentence or phrase that tells them what the topic of the paragraph is. They could also highlight the words that link the paragraphs (see Chapter 1).

- **Photocopiable page 115 'Information paragraphs'**

Here the children develop their understanding of how a non-fiction information text can be organised into paragraphs that split it into separate topics. Explain that adding headings will help readers to know what the text is about and to find the information they are looking for.

Further ideas

- **Headlines:** Children write newspaper-style headlines for paragraphs of text from well-known stories, for example: *Mother and son too poor to buy food*, *Son sent to market with last cow*, *Son swaps cow for beans*, *Mother furious in bean swap row*, *Huge beanstalk appears in garden*, and so on.
- **My story paragraphs:** Children read through their own stories with a partner and decide how they have used paragraphs (for example, for topics in a description or to separate events). They choose a story to edit, marking any places where text could be split into separate paragraphs.
- **Speed read:** Make two different copies of an information text: one with headings and the other with headings deleted. Split the class in half, matched for reading ability and working in groups of three. Ask them to find specific pieces of information, such as the answers to questions. Once the group finds the information, they hold up a card. Did the group who found it first have the text with headings? Children should find that information is much easier to find with headings.

Digital content

On the digital component you will find:

- Printable versions of all three photocopiable pages.
- Answers to 'Story paragraphs' and 'Paragraph topics'.

Using paragraphs in writing

Story paragraphs

In stories, paragraphs can be useful for separating events.

■ Read the story below. Using the table, write notes about the events in each paragraph. The first has been done for you.

The captive

It was morning. Meera knew that because daylight was creeping through a little gap at the side of the door. What door? This was no door she knew and this was not where she had fallen asleep. Was it a dream? No. Her arm felt sore. She felt the sore part. What had happened to it?

Meera got up and went to open the door. It was locked. She sat down and tried to think. She looked around the room as the daylight pushed through the gap. She had been sleeping on a mattress on a dusty wooden floor.

Her feet were bare but she was dressed in her jeans and jumper. She looked for her shoes and socks. Which shoes had she been wearing? But there were no shoes in the little room – just a bed.

Then she heard a man's voice, then a woman answering, somewhere not far from the door. Who were they? She strained her ears to listen.

She caught a few words: "Twenty thousand…", "No, not enough…", "…want her back…", "…police", "…they'll pay…", "If they don't, they'll never get her back."

Paragraph 1	Meera wakes, wonders where she is, sore arm, how hurt arm
Paragraph 2	
Paragraph 3	
Paragraph 4	
Paragraph 5	

Name:

Using paragraphs in writing

Paragraph topics

- Read the passage.
- Then complete the table to show what each paragraph is about.

Mr Crumble

Mr Crumble was absent-minded. Sometimes he put on odd shoes and didn't notice until someone told him that one was black and the other was brown. His socks never matched because he lost so many – never a pair, but always one from each pair.

His brother once said that there must be a secret place where all Mr Crumble's socks were hiding and that if only he could find it he could make pairs of all his brother's socks. But his sister said that was no use because by then Mr Crumble would have lost all their partners. She said he should always buy the same kind of socks – then whatever socks he put on would always be a matching pair.

While everyone else was worrying about all the things he got wrong, Mr Crumble's mind was taken up with more interesting things: it was full of ideas for inventions. It didn't matter if his socks were odd or his jumper was on back-to-front or he had no milk in the fridge when he was busy inventing.

"Inventors don't have to be absent-minded," said Mr Crumble's brother one day. "It's not a special qualification for the job."

Mr Crumble smiled. He knew that. He wasn't trying to be a typical inventor. It was just that it helped if his mind wasn't cluttered up with socks and shoes and milk and things like that. His mind had plenty of space for inventing.

Paragraph	What the paragraph is about
1	
2	
3	
4	
5	

Using paragraphs in writing

Information paragraphs

■ Work with a partner. Read this text from a geography book and discuss how to organise it into paragraphs.
■ Draw a box around each paragraph. In the margin, write a heading for each paragraph.

Paragraph headings	
	China is a very big country. Its area is about 9.6 million square kilometres, making it the world's second-largest country by land area. Russia is the largest. A third of the country is covered with mountains. These include the Himalayas, which also stretch into Afghanistan, India, Pakistan, Myanmar, Nepal and Bhutan. Mount Everest, the tallest mountain in the world, is on the border of China and Nepal. There are several rivers flowing through China. The most important are the Yangtze and the Yellow River. The Yangtze is the third largest river in the world. China's largest city by population is Shanghai but its capital is Beijing. The largest by area is Guangzhou. Shanghai has the world's busiest container port. It is on the coast at the mouth of the Yangtze River. China has a population of more than 1.35 billion people. This is the largest of all the countries in the world.

Organising sentences and texts

Objective

Consider how sentences and texts are organised.

Background knowledge

There can be different levels of organisation within a text, for example: sections, chapters, paragraphs, sentences and clauses. This organisation can be based on different purposes; the purposes that will be the most familiar to children are time/sequence or topic. Other possibilities include comparison, contrast, points in an argument or persuasion, evaluation and exemplification. Each purpose will tend to use certain linking words or phrases for cohesion.

Activities

- **Photocopiable page 117 'All in a sentence'**
This activity challenges the children to put a given set of information into one sentence, using clauses, expanding noun phases and finding ways to link these. There are different ways in which each sentence could be written. Children could share their answers.
- **Photocopiable page 118 'All in a paragraph'**
Here the children organise sentences into paragraphs based around topics. They first have to identify the topics and then group the sentences around them, arranging them in an order that makes sense. Having completed this, the task of adding words or phrases to link the sentences could be started as a shared activity, where necessary, using the whiteboard.
- **Photocopiable page 119 'All in a text'**
The children organise a set of paragraphs into an appropriate order and then insert words or phrases to link the paragraphs. There is no 'right answer' except that there is a clear introductory paragraph, which should come first.

Further ideas

- **My sentences:** Children edit their own writing, checking their use of nouns/pronouns. Have they avoided repetition? Have they used pronouns in a way that makes clear what they mean? Could they combine sentences by expanding noun phrases?
- **My paragraphs:** Children re-read their own extended pieces of non-fiction writing, focusing on their use of paragraphing. How well have they used paragraphs to separate topics? How could they improve their use of paragraphs?
- **Paragraph sorting:** Cut a leaflet into its separate paragraphs for the children, working in threes, to put in order and to identify words that link paragraphs and sentences.

Digital content

On the digital component you will find:

- Printable versions of all three photocopiable pages.
- Answers to 'All in a sentence'.

Name:

Organising sentences and texts

All in a sentence

- Read the information in each box.
- Then try to write it all in one sentence. One has been done for you.

Newcastle is a big city. It is in north-east England. It is on the banks of the River Tyne.	Newcastle is a big city on the banks of the River Tyne in north-east England.
I bought the book in town. Ross said it was an exciting adventure story.	
This was my grandma's jewel box. That's why I like to use it. I keep some bracelets in it.	
I turned over a stone. It was on the beach. I found a coin. It was under the stone. It was silver. It was old.	
My dad is very tall. He has dark hair. His eyes are brown. He has a beard. Mum doesn't like his beard.	
We're going on holiday in July. We're going to Spain. We're going for two weeks. Then we're going to Wales.	
Dan's rabbit escaped from its hutch. He had forgotten to close the door. He had been cleaning the hutch. It happened on Sunday. The rabbit is still missing.	

Name:

All in a paragraph

Here are some sentences from a leaflet about hedgehogs.

■ Work with a partner. Read the sentences and decide what the main topics are. Then cut out the sentences and group them into three paragraphs, in order.

■ On a separate piece of paper, rewrite the sentences, using extra words to link them.

In October, hedgehogs begin to prepare for the winter, when they hibernate from about November to March.
If they eat slug pellets and pesticides they are poisoned and may die.
They will also eat frogs, toads, birds' eggs, roots, berries and other fruits.
When faced with danger, hedgehogs curl into a ball.
Hedgehogs are mammals.
Between 50,000 and 100,000 hedgehogs are killed on the roads each year, but many more are killed in other ways.
It is illegal to kill them, but their greatest threat is from humans, who sometimes kill them accidentally.
They have a covering of spines.
Hedgehogs feed mainly on insects, snails and worms.
They might roll into steep-sided ponds and drown or become trapped.
They build up body fat through feeding on small animals such as beetles, caterpillars, slugs and worms.
They build a nest from twigs and leaves in any suitable area – usually on the ground.
They hibernate in wood piles and are burnt when fires are lit to burn garden waste.
Their spines are not poisonous.
They can get caught in netting or discarded food tins and suffocate or starve to death.
Their spines protect them from predators, such as eagles, foxes, owls, polecats and snakes.

Organising sentences and texts

All in a text

- Work with a partner.
- Cut out these paragraphs from a tourist information brochure.
- Decide what order to put the paragraphs in. Then glue them onto a sheet of paper.
- Add some words or phrases to link the paragraphs to one another. You might need to cross out some words first.

The main industry is wine-making. It gives the landscape its character. Fields with rows of vines stretch for miles. The grapes are harvested in September.
Most markets are held in shady avenues of plane trees – usually in the morning, starting very early and ending at midday.
For the children there's a big fairground at Valras Plage and Aqualand at the Cap d'Agde, with pools, water chutes and much more.
Languedoc-Roussillon is a region in the South of France, with a coast on the Mediterranean Sea to the south and mountains (the Pyrenees) to the west. The Canal du Midi crosses the region.
Languedoc-Roussillon has large cities, such as Béziers and Narbonne, and many villages with markets selling local foods.
If you're looking for beaches with parasols and sun loungers to hire, try the Cap d'Agde or Valras Plage.
Nearly every town has its fete, with traditional music, dance and costumes – as well as plenty of delicious local foods.

Cohesion in writing

Objective

Write clearly and cohesively within sentences and across paragraphs.

Writing focus

Building on previous activities, this section encourages children to consider how their sentences take shape, and how they can organise these sentences into paragraphs, ensuring cohesion throughout their writing.

Skills to writing

- **Noun planning**

Nouns support planning. When thinking ahead to a report text, children can structure their writing by thinking of the nouns related to their subject. Those who haven't made a start on writing about a subject will often suddenly gain ideas when asked to list a set of nouns associated with that subject. Nouns can be especially useful in planning and structuring report texts. A good first step to writing a report text can be to think of the 'nouns within the noun'. For example, for a subject such as 'The playground', the children can make a list of all the nouns associated with it (benches, a climbing frame, a tree, litter bins and so on). Using 'a' or 'the' before each word will help the children to check they are using the right sort of word. The children can then use the list, putting it into a logical order, and fleshing it out to create their report. Using a 'mind map' or 'spider gram' the children can group the nouns (see photocopiable page 122 'Nouns for a report'). Each group can then become the basis for a paragraph.

- **Cohesion**

Reference is one of the ways in which writers hold their texts together. It can be seen in this very sentence, where the opening 'it' made a link between this sentence and the word 'reference' earlier in the paragraph. As children progress through Key Stage 2 and their writing grows from sentences to a number of paragraphs, the knitting together of the text can be reinforced through ensuring that pronouns are used with clarity.

Activities

- **Photocopiable page 122 'Nouns for a report'**

This page can be used in connection with work in another subject. It provides a format to help children to plan a report around the nouns they list. You could ask children to write a list of nouns on a separate piece of paper before using the diagram to organise them into groups and to link the groups together. Remind them that they can add circles if necessary. Their completed diagram will help them to organise their report into paragraphs.

- **Photocopiable page 123 'Sentences for a report'**

Children should first have completed page 122. Page 123 provides a format and hints to help children to organise their groups of nouns into sentences (within the paragraphs that will naturally have formed as they listed their report nouns). They could continue in the same way to write more paragraphs for their report.

Write on

- **Opening ambiguity**

While it's vital to ensure clear reference in the use of pronouns, a bit of ambiguity can be used to good effect. Opening lines like *He sat bolt upright* or *"What was that?" she whispered*, act as hooks to a reader. We want to know who 'he' is, what's going on and what 'that' was. In their narrative writing, children can be encouraged to open a story or a chapter with an ambiguous pronoun that will make the reader want to know to what the pronouns refer.

- **Ambiguous pronouns**

Children can play with ambiguous pronouns in their writing. Lines such as *The boy ran up to the dog. He bit him*, leave us wondering who bit whom. Children could try using this idea in a short piece of writing. The basic idea is to script a conversation between two people where the use of a pronoun causes confusion. Someone says something clear and then uses pronouns. For example: *The boy ran up to the dog, and he bit him* and a listener responds with confusion: *The boy bit the dog?* This isn't easy, but children like the idea.

- **Creepy door**

Children can both write and record their own creepy texts, similar to the one on photocopiable page 107 'The door', and then record these. Sustain the mystery through the ambiguous language – mystery pronouns really help: *He looked up the staircase. Was she up there?* As the children produce an audio version, they need to ask how they will modulate the voice of the teller and what sound effects they could add.

- **Pick a paragraph**

As a whole class or individually, look back at a non-fiction paragraph that the children have written. Choose a paragraph that isn't the opening introduction. Ask children what the paragraph is about – its topic and whether it keeps to the topic or some parts should be moved. This will involve reading other paragraphs. The children could give each paragraph a subheading that says what it is about. This will help them to focus on the text of the chapter and decide what doesn't belong in that paragraph, possibly moving it to another paragraph or creating a new paragraph altogether.

- **Just one paragraph**

Read the paragraph chosen for the previous activity and, through inserting words and redrafting sentences, refine this one paragraph until children think it reads as well as possible. Encourage them to consider the nouns and pronouns to check for ambiguity or repetition – changing pronouns to nouns to avoid the former and vice versa for the latter.

Digital content

On the digital component you will find:

- Printable versions of both photocopiable pages.

Name:

Nouns for a report

- Use this page to help you to collect ideas for a report.
- Write the subject of your report in the oval at the centre of the diagram below. Write one of your nouns in a circle. Then add any nouns that link to it. Write other nouns in the remaining circles and add any linked nouns.
- Draw lines where you want to link the ideas in the circles.

Sentences for a report

- You need your 'Nouns for a report' page. Write the name of your report.
- Decide which group of nouns you will use in the first paragraph (Introduction). Use these nouns in sentences. Write the sentences in the box for paragraph 1. Use words and phrases that link the sentences.
- Do the same for the next two paragraphs. Write the paragraph topic in the space.

Report name: ____________________

Paragraph 1 Introduction	
Paragraph 2 Topic:	
Paragraph 3 Topic:	

Chapter 6

Punctuation

Introduction

This chapter revisits punctuation marks the children have learned in previous years as well as those introduced in previous chapters of this book. For further practice, please see the 'Punctuation' section of the Year 4 workbook.

Poster notes

Punctuation (page 125)
The list of punctuation marks encountered in the chapter is complemented by a list of sentences. In the various sentences, children will find examples of the punctuation marks referred to in the list.
Inverted commas (page 126)
This poster can be used to consolidate children's previous learning about punctuating direct speech. It is useful to remind them that any words or punctuation marks that would be written in a speech bubble should be written between the two sets of inverted commas.

In this chapter

Revisiting punctuation page 127	Identify and consolidate understanding of basic punctuation.
Direct speech page 131	Revisit the use of inverted commas to indicate direct speech.
Punctuating direct speech page 135	Punctuate direct speech correctly.
Adverbials and commas page 139	Use a comma after an adverbial that precedes a verb.
Using a range of punctuation in writing page 143	Apply punctuation accurately in writing.

Vocabulary

Children should already know:
adverbial, full stop, question mark, exclamation mark, comma, apostrophe, inverted commas
In Year 4 children need to know:
adverbial

Punctuation

Punctuation

■ **The capital letter**
The children were messing about.

■ **The full stop**
We made spinners at school**.**

■ **The question mark**
How do you make a spinner**?**

■ **Commas in lists**
To make a spinner you will need paper**,** sticky tape**,** string and tissue paper.

■ **Inverted commas**
Sam said, “Don’t jump on the sofa.”

■ **The exclamation mark**
Don’t jump on the sofa**!**

■ **The comma after an adverbial that comes before a verb**
In the meantime**,** I did my homework.

■ **The apostrophe for possession**
Three boys’ answers followed one girl’s question.

Punctuation

Inverted commas

Inverted commas surround words that are spoken.

Put **punctuation marks** at the end of spoken words before the inverted commas.

Put **inverted commas** before and after the spoken words.

Emma asked Joshua, "What do you call a cross between an ice cream and a football team**?**"

Joshua **replied**, "*I don't know.*"

"***Aston Vanilla!***" said Emma.

Put a **comma** after a word or phrase that comes before the spoken words.

Revisiting punctuation

Objective

Identify and consolidate understanding of basic punctuation.

Background knowledge

These activities provide practice in the use of capital letters, full stops, question marks and exclamation marks for demarcating sentences; commas in lists and apostrophes to mark possession or omission. (The capital letter is, strictly speaking, not a punctuation mark, but is taught at the same time as the full stop.)

Punctuation emerges through children's writing as it develops. Children will often write sentences that should include certain items of punctuation but omit the actual marks. The emphasis here is on activities that help to draw out the individual child's awareness of punctuation.

Activities

- **Photocopiable page 128 'Punctuation hunt'**

This activity reinforces children's previous learning about punctuation by asking them to read text in newspapers and magazines and to identify punctuation marks and explain their purposes in these contexts. Some children may need help in clarifying the task that a particular punctuation mark is performing once they have identified it in the text. This becomes clearer if they delete the punctuation mark and notice the difference this makes.

- **Photocopiable page 129 'Check these out'**

The sentences provided in this activity will accommodate the use of capital letters, full stops, question marks, commas, apostrophes for possession or omission and exclamation marks.

- **Photocopiable page 130 'My punctuation'**

This page provides a framework for children to collect their own uses of some of the punctuation marks covered up to this point. It involves some copying, as the idea is that children should look through their writing to find real and uncontrived examples of their personal use of these punctuation marks. They should copy the examples they find and put them on the chart. As children collect a range of different punctuation marks, the task provides a record of their progress in this aspect of writing and will be useful in setting targets for their writing.

Further ideas

- **Popular punctuation marks:** Ask the children to look at different texts to see if any punctuation marks appear more often in some text types than in others, for example: comic stories can contain numerous exclamation marks; exam papers often have many question marks.
- **Race to find:** Give the children a three-minute challenge. Explain that, working in groups of three with newspaper cuttings, they have to try to find as many punctuation marks as they can within the time limit.
- **Use it like this:** Children make up their own examples of how to use each of the punctuation marks covered in the activities. They could present them in a poster.

Digital content

On the digital component you will find:

- Printable versions of all three photocopiable pages.
- Answers to 'Check these out'.
- Interactive version of 'Check these out'.

Name:

Punctuation hunt

■ Look through a magazine and collect examples of five different types of punctuation. Cut out the pieces of text and paste them into the boxes. Write an explanation of what the punctuation marks are doing underneath the cuttings.

THE NEW BUS ROUTE WILL BE USEFUL FOR TOURISTS, SCHOOLCHILDREN, OLDER PEOPLE AND ANYONE WHO DOESN'T DRIVE. comma – separates items in a list	

Check these out

■ Rewrite these sentences with the correct punctuation.

i can see my friend

can we go to the park

is it raining

we are going to the park

my favourite colours are red purple pink and orange

ive just been to see Sunils new bike

can you see my friend

Harrys mums new shop sells ladies and childrens shoes but not mens shoes

stop look and listen before you cross the road

Name:

Revisiting punctuation

My punctuation

■ Look through your writing for examples of different punctuation marks you have used. Jot down the sentences in which you used them.

Punctuation mark	**My sentence**

SCHOLASTIC
www.scholastic.co.uk

Direct speech

Objective

Revisit the use of inverted commas to indicate direct speech.

Background knowledge

Children will have learned in Year 3 that inverted commas separate speech from the rest of the sentence. Here they begin to use them in sentences. They could first use inverted commas to help them to identify the words spoken by characters in simple picture story books. They should notice that the spoken words are enclosed within a pair of inverted commas. This section focuses mainly on the use of inverted commas to enclose spoken words in text. The main teaching point is that inverted commas enclose the spoken words. Punctuation at the end of the spoken words (before the closing inverted commas) is introduced in these activities, but it is dealt with in more detail in the next section.

Activities

- **Photocopiable page 132 'Knock, knock'**

This page presents a series of 'Knock, knock' jokes that consist of dialogue without any reporting clauses. This helps children to focus on the use of two sets of inverted commas to surround the spoken words and their final punctuation. It is useful to point out the position of the final punctuation within the inverted commas.

- **Photocopiable page 133 'Inverted commas'**

As they try to demarcate the words in the sentences, children will need to figure out which words were actually spoken. The reporting clauses precede the spoken words, providing an opportunity to introduce the positioning of punctuation that ends the spoken words – always before the closing inverted commas.

- **Photocopiable page 134 'Pick an argument'**

Children need to work on this in groups of six or fewer. They cut out cards paper and these are placed face downwards in the middle of the group. Ask them to write one of the arguments shown on the cards using lots of speech, clearly demarcated. Ask them to begin with who is speaking before writing what the person says (reporting clause preceding the spoken words): *Mum said, "Calm down!", Tortoise answered, "No...", Saucepan replied*, and so on, and remind children to use other punctuation correctly, in addition to inverted commas. Once this is clear, everyone picks a card and has to start writing. If there is time they could repeat this for another argument of their choice.

Further ideas

- **Comic contexts:** Taking a conversation that takes place in a comic story as their starting point, children can look at how much of a comic story depends on the pictures. They can try recording the dialogue from some of the pictures separately and see how much sense it makes standing alone. They could then look in the comic story and see what the context of the picture contributed to the speech. Ask them to begin each new set of spoken words in a way that shows who is speaking (with the reporting clause preceding the spoken words).
- **Plays and pictures:** Children can try turning a scripted text, such as a playscript, into a comic-strip story. They will need to account for who said what to whom, and should draw the characters with their speech bubbles and the final punctuation.

Digital content

On the digital component you will find:

- Printable versions of all three photocopiable pages.
- Answers to 'Knock, knock' and 'Inverted commas'.
- Interactive version of 'Inverted commas'.

Name:

Direct speech

Knock, knock

■ Add inverted commas at the beginning and end of each set of spoken words.

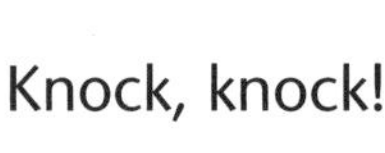

Knock, knock!
Who's there?
Juno.
Juno who?
Juno who just knocked.

Knock, knock!
Who's there?
Neil.
Neil who?
Neil on the mat to see through the letter box.

Knock, knock!
Who's there?
Wayne.
Wayne who?
Wayne a ton can be a problem!

Direct speech

Inverted commas

■ These lines have lost their inverted commas. Can you rewrite them putting the inverted commas in?

Sam said Quick, hide the map.

Josh said Help me clean up this mess.

The teacher asked Where are you going?

The boy asked the teacher Shall I tidy the art corner?

Mum said Abby would you help me to change this wheel?

Abby said OK, where's the spare wheel?

Mum said There it is – beside the car.

Name:

Direct speech

Pick an argument

■ Cut out these cards and pick an argument.

Two people arguing over which one of them was the first to get to the supermarket checkout.

A mum arguing with her child who is being really stroppy in a cafe.

A hare arguing with a tortoise about which one of them would win a race.

A driving instructor telling his pupil off for driving so badly and the pupil disagreeing.

A pot arguing with a saucepan about which of them is the most useful.

A dog arguing with its owner that the walk they just went on was too short.

Punctuating direct speech

Objective

Punctuate direct speech correctly.

Background knowledge

These activities introduce the use of a comma after the reporting clause, where this precedes the spoken words, and end punctuation within the inverted commas. End punctuation always precedes the closing inverted commas. A question mark or exclamation mark remains unchanged, even if followed by a reporting clause: *"Would you tell me when we reach the station, please?" asked the girl.* A full stop changes to a comma if followed by a reporting clause and the reporting clause begins with a lower-case letter: *"Next stop – the station," said the bus driver.*

Activities

- **Photocopiable page 136 'Opening direct speech'**
This activity focuses on the comma that precedes direct speech where there is a reporting clause before the spoken words. It also provides an opportunity to consider different words for 'said', although children should use 'said' if this is the most appropriate. It is important to emphasise that the comma comes after 'said', or its equivalent, but before the opening inverted commas, and also that new spoken words always begin with a capital letter.
- **Photocopiable page 137 'Closing direct speech'**
Here the focus is on punctuation at the end of direct speech. This is omitted and children are asked to identify places where it is omitted and to insert the punctuation that concludes the spoken words and then the inverted commas. It is important to emphasise that the final inverted commas always come after the punctuation that concludes the spoken words.
- **Photocopiable page 138 'Helping the reader'**
This tightly written dialogue is an example of Philip Ridley's excellent presentation of speech in his novels. Children should locate inverted commas and notice that, where a new piece of direct speech begins the line is indented. These help the reader to follow the dialogue and to understand the text.

Further ideas

- **Finding:** Children can look through different types of text that contain speech for examples of direct speech, such as history books that might narrate the events of a particular time, modern novels and different levels of a reading scheme.
- **Play to text:** Read passages from playscripts and ask the children to identify the spoken words. Ask how these would be written if it were a story rather than a playscript. They can then write a short scene from a play as a story. This could include adding narrative to the dialogue. Children could begin to indent each new piece of direct speech.
- **Listen and write:** Children listen to short passages of dialogue (radio, television, online) and write it down, showing who said what. They will need to insert reporting clauses.

Digital content

On the digital component you will find:

- Printable versions of all three photocopiable pages.
- Answers to 'Opening direct speech' and 'Closing direct speech'.

Name:

Punctuating direct speech

Opening direct speech

■ Rewrite the text messages below as a conversation, using inverted commas and commas.

■ For each one, use a different word for 'said'.

Can you come to my house after school?
Jack

OK. I'll ask my mum.
Lian

Dad said he'd take us tenpin bowling. OK?
Jack

Yes. Great.
Lian

I forgot to tell you. Dad said he'd take you home.
Jack

Mum said yes, and thanks!
Lian

Jack asked Lian, " ____

Lian answered ____

Closing direct speech

Punctuation marks at the end of direct speech always come before the inverted commas:

> Raj asked, "What time is it, please?"
>
> Tia answered, "It's six o'clock."
>
> "What time is it please?" asked Raj.
>
> "It's six o'clock," answered Tia.

■ Put in the punctuation marks at the ends of the direct speech in this news report.

To free or not to free

Motorists in Jeepton are split over the town council's plan to make parking free.

"It will bring in visitors who will spend money in the town said Councillor Mary Moore. "This will be good for local businesses

"People working here will take up the parking spaces all day, so visitors will find it even harder to park said one local man.

Another added, "It's not expensive in any case

"You might not find it expensive complained another. "For pensioners every penny counts

"Doesn't the council need the money from parking asked Anna Smallcar. "They'll just charge higher council tax

"Yes agreed her neighbour Gemma Bigcar. We'll be paying for the visitors

"That's right said another local woman, adding, "The council will make sure they don't lose anything

Name:

Punctuating direct speech

Helping the reader

■ Look at this passage from *Kasper in the Glitter*. Kasper has entered the city called 'The Gloom' and has met Jingo. Circle the punctuation that helps the reader.

■ Discuss with a partner how new paragraphs help.

'This way, if you please, Master Kasper,' said Jingo.

He led Kasper into a long and gloomy alleyway.

Their footsteps echoed all round them.

Now that Jingo didn't have the basket to carry, he wasn't quite sure what to do with his hands. To keep them occupied, he picked up his dirty jacket tails, muttered, 'Gracious me!' then brushed them clean. When they were clean, he let them fall back to the ground, whereupon they soon got dirty again, so he picked them up once more, muttered another 'Gracious me!' and brushed them all over again.

Kasper watched Jingo in amazement for a while, then looked round the alleyway.

The City doesn't look very sparkling, thought Kasper. All I can see at the moment are leaking drainpipes, broken windows and piles of rubbish. And this alleyway smells revolting. It needs a good dose of bleach and disinfectant.

'And now, Master Kasper,' began Jingo, his voice bubbling with excitement, 'it's my turn to surprise you.'

'It is?' said Kasper.

'Have you any idea who I'm going to cook the pie for?'

'None at all.'

'Master Kasper,' he said 'you are holding the ingredients that will make the favourite pie of ...' And here he took a deep breath so he could say it loudly and with pride, 'The King.'

'The King?' said Kasper. 'The King of what?'

'The King of The Gloom, of course,' Jingo replied. 'KING STREETWISE!'

And his voice echoed up and down the alley.

'STREETWISE ... TREETWISE ... REETWISE ... EETWISE ... TWISE ... WISE ... ISE ... SSSSS.'

Kasper in the Glitter
Philip Ridley

Adverbials and commas

Objective

Use a comma after an adverbial that precedes a verb.

Background knowledge

These activities consolidate previous work on the use of commas. It is useful to remind children about their previous learning about adverbials and where they can be placed in a sentence. (See Chapter 4.) Adverbials that precede the verb (fronted adverbials) are usually, but not always followed by a comma. Note that children do not need to know the term 'fronted adverbials' – just that adverbials can appear before the verb.

Activities

- **Photocopiable page 140 'Comma hunt'**

This activity requires children to work in pairs to decide where, in a passage, there should be commas and to explain to one another why each comma is needed. It focuses on commas in lists, and commas following a reporting clause that introduces spoken words.

- **Photocopiable page 141 'More commas'**

This introduces the use of a comma after a fronted adverbial (an adverbial that comes before the verb it modifies). It is useful first to remind the children of their previous learning about adverbials – the job they do in a sentence – and to begin by reading some sentences containing adverbials that follow the verbs they modify. Ask the children to identify the adverbials. They should then be able to spot where to add commas in the sentences provided. It is useful to display some practice sentences on the whiteboard, where the adverbials can be moved so that they precede the verbs (with capital letters adjusted accordingly). Children could practise moving the adverbials so that they precede the verbs in sentences in this way. Read some of the sentences aloud, try adding a comma after the adverbial and encourage the children to say whether the comma is needed.

- **Photocopiable page 142 'Turnaround'**

Here, the children rewrite sentences containing adverbials so that the adverbial precedes the verb. They then add a comma if needed. As for the 'practice sentences' for the previous activity, children could begin by rewriting sentences with the adverbials moved so that they precede the verb. Ask them to read the changed sentences aloud and to say whether they think a comma would help to make the meaning clear. Children should then be able to decide where to add commas in the sentences provided.

Further ideas

- **Add an adverbial:** Children add adverbials to sentences provided, with the purpose of adding information about how, when, where or why the action took place. They choose where to add the adverbial and could experiment with different adverbials to add information about how, where, when or why an action takes place.
- **Back to front:** Children decide what difference it makes to the meaning or emphasis of a sentence when the position of the adverbial is changed. They could experiment by typing their sentence on a computer and then copying and pasting sections of the sentence to produce different versions. They then choose the one they prefer.
- **Advertised adverbial:** Children listen or look for adverbials in advertisements, select sentences containing them, write the sentences and underline the adverbial, noticing whether it is before or after the verb.

Digital content

On the digital component you will find:

- Printable versions of all three photocopiable pages.
- Answers to all three photocopiable pages.
- Interactive version of 'More commas'.

Name:

Adverbials and commas

Comma hunt

The comma key on the computer is not working, so all the commas have been missed out of this passage.

- Working with a partner, put commas where you think they should be.
- Explain to one another why you think commas should be in these places.

The circus

There was once a man called Russ who worked in a car factory. One day the factory closed down. He had no job. He had to find work to pay for electricity gas food and clothes.

Every day Russ had a shower put on clean clothes polished his shoes and went to look for work.

One day he saw a circus coming to town. He thought "I've never worked in a circus but I'll try anything."

He went to see the circus manager.

The circus manager said "My gorilla has died. If you will wear his skin and pretend to be a gorilla I'll pay you."

Russ didn't like the sound of this job but he said "Yes. I'll do it."

Russ put on the gorilla's skin and pretended to be a gorilla. He swung from bar to bar ate bananas and made gorilla noises. The circus manager smiled.

Russ swung very high missed the bar and crashed to the floor of the cage. Unfortunately he crashed through the bars into the tiger's cage below. The tiger looked at him growled and came loping towards him. Russ yelled "Get me out of here!"

"Shut up you fool" said the tiger. "If you're not careful we'll both lose our jobs."

The tiger chased Russ. He climbed the bars swung into his cage ate a banana and made monkey noises at the tiger. The audience stood up cheered clapped and called for more.

More commas

Sometimes an adverbial comes before the verb in a sentence. Often it is followed by a comma.

Every Saturday morning at ten o'clock, I play rugby.

■ Look for the adverbials that come before the verbs in the sentences below. Put commas after them.

After school may I borrow your toolbox?

Tomorrow I'll come and visit you.

In the last three years she hasn't written to me once.

Under the car park they found the skeleton of Richard III.

At the top of Mount Everest there are crowds of climbers.

Nowadays it isn't a remote and difficult place to get to.

Right up to that day the old woman had been waiting for her son to be found.

At last she could see him again.

During times of heavy rainfall please do not use this bridge.

Because of Simon's short legs people thought he couldn't run fast.

However Simon proved them wrong by winning the 100 metres.

Name:

Adverbials and commas

Turnaround

- Work with a partner. Look for the adverbials in these sentences.
- Rewrite the sentences with the adverbials in front of the verbs. Remember to put a comma where it is needed.

The front door was open to our surprise.

____

It was definitely closed this morning.

____

Dad remembered checking it at 9 o'clock.

____

Someone had opened it in the meantime.

____

Mum phoned the police on her mobile.

____

A police car arrived in a few minutes.

____

They found a burglar under the stairs.

____

Using a range of punctuation in writing

Objective

Apply punctuation accurately in writing.

Writing focus

Building on previous activities, this section consolidates children's use of punctuation in writing.

Skills to writing

- **Checklist**

The children should start to maintain their own punctuation checklist, checking off their own deployment of the range of marks in their writing. This should be handled with a sense of progression, with the sentence ending marks – full stop, question mark and exclamation mark – tackled first. Then, within sentences, children should target the use of apostrophes for possession and omission and inverted commas. Parallel with this they should look to use commas in lists, as well as other places: following a reporting clause before direct speech; replacing a full stop before a reporting clause that follows direct speech; and following an adverbial that comes before the verb.

- **Drama**

There is an integral link between the effective teaching of inverted commas and drama. Of course, it's not just about punctuation. It's also about content. As part of the process of devising and demarcating conversations, children need to have them. They could enact a scene where a child is trying to persuade a teacher or nagging a parent, and then write a dialogue based on their scene.

- **Conversations aloud**

When reading texts that contain speech, encourage the class to use the text sometimes as a script, figuring out which lines belong to which speaker and then having individuals take his or her role. Children become better attuned to the liveliness of speech in text when they hear the lines turned into a conversation.

- **Quotations**

Reported speech is not restricted to narrative writing. Although it has a clear part to play in recount texts, it can also figure in almost any text type, for example, many popular science books are enlivened with quotations from the scientists whose ideas populate the pages. As children write explanation and report texts, they can be encouraged to listen out for interesting lines to quote in their text from whatever resources stimulate their writing. To discourage the copying of entire paragraphs, suggest that quotes should be short, one-sentence items. Also make it clear that good quotes are sharp and memorable. The important point is to enclose quotations and their punctuation in inverted commas.

- **Adverbials in action**

Adverbials feature strongly in sports commentaries and reports, particularly games involving changes of position and speed, such as football or rugby. Children could identify those they hear in a recorded commentary on a football or rugby match. These might not be in complete sentences, but could be displayed on the whiteboard and completed as sentences, with adverbials before the verbs. Others could be rearranged, moving adverbials so that they come before the verbs.

Activities

- **Photocopiable page 145 'Perfect punctuation'**

This provides a passage with some punctuation missing. The children identify places that need punctuation and choose from a set of given punctuation marks (full stops, apostrophes, and commas). They punctuate the passage and share this with their group, noticing any differences. They might need help in identifying any variations in meaning caused by different punctuation.

- **Photocopiable page 146 'Words in your mouth'**

This encourages the children to consider how punctuation can help to identify spoken words in text. They read a passage and put in the missing inverted commas. Afterwards they could use it as the basis of a modern Goldilocks story with dialogue.

Write on

- **Character talk**

Use talk as a way of developing characters in narrative writing. Ask the children to try to put the things we need to know about a character into their speech. If they have a guilty secret, don't have the writer tell us in a plain sentence (Josh was really a robot.). Have the character confess (*Josh said, "Mum, there's something you should know."*). While doing this, characters can also be given a catchphrase or some other verbal feature.

- **One-line speech**

Children will often write speech in big chunks, unlike the exchange that would normally take place between two people. This activity explores the more interactive nature of conversation. Ask children to think of a context in which two people would have a discussion – be it informative, argumentative or moaning. Whatever the content, ask them to span the conversation over a page, using short lines rather than big paragraphs of speech. One character must interrupt or question the other.

- **Argument**

Children like writing arguments. They have usually been in or near one recently and can recall how they go. Local and national news will usually provide examples: sporting issues such as the behaviour of footballers on the pitch, the use of technology by referees; environmental/technological/economic issues such as sources of fuel, the building of new roads, railways, airports or tunnels or new housing developments.

- **Conversations**

Write the conversations of history. Find a historical topic that children have covered and write up, for example, the exchange Drake had as he was supposed to finish his bowls game and fight the Armada. Think of other topics of conversation that fit in with topic work.

- **Speech punctuation**

Speech can provide a good focus for developing children's use of punctuation. As they imagine characters in a narrative, or develop speech in a recount, ask them to look at the way certain punctuation marks can stimulate their writing.

In the course of writing a conversation: *Could one character ask another a question? Will a character make a sudden exclamation – and if so, why? As a character says one thing, could they add a bit of extra detail (punctuated by placing a comma where it is needed)? When giving a bit of extra detail, could one character make a short digression, embedded in a clause?* The aim here is not to see punctuation as a forced inclusion, but rather to use it as a stimulus to suggest how to develop a piece of writing. This could be fiction or poetry – using punctuation to create effects – or a persuasive letter in which punctuation is used to emphasise a point or to make comparisons.

Digital content

On the digital component you will find:
- Printable versions of both photocopiable pages.
- Answers to 'Words in your mouth'.

Using a range of punctuation in writing

Perfect punctuation

■ The passage below has some punctuation marks. Make its meaning clearer by adding additional punctuation marks where you think they are needed.

■ When you add a full stop, don't forget that the next sentence starts with a capital letter.

. full stop
' apostrophe for possession
, comma

The Romans land in Britain

In the year 55BCE in late August 12,000 of Julius Caesars army of Roman soldiers landed on the south coast of Britain before they landed an army of Britons had spotted the Roman ships and was ready to fight off the invaders they had swords and shields the Romans had swords shields and metal armour

The Britons charged down the beach to where the Romans ships were coming in this forced the Romans to fight in the water the Romans won the battle but they didn't stay in Britain the next year Julius Caesar came back once again Caesars army beat the British however they had to leave because there was trouble in Gaul (France) this was part of Caesars empire

After 90 years another Roman emperor came to Britain his name was Claudius Claudiuss soldiers had heard what good fighters the British were but the Romans had better weapons armour horses and elephants the elephants scared the British soldiers they had never seen elephants

This time the Romans stayed over the years they built roads towns and forts they traded with the British settled alongside them and lived peacefully here

Name:

Using a range of punctuation in writing

Words in your mouth

The conversation below is difficult to read because the inverted commas are missing.

- Add inverted commas where you think they are needed.

Goldilocks under arrest

Well, said the police officer to Goldilocks. You're under arrest for breaking and entering. Anything you say may be used as evidence.

Oh, no, said Goldilocks. I was lost and this house looked so nice that I came in. I was hungry and I didn't think anyone would mind if I ate a bowl of porridge.

It was my porridge said a voice from behind the police officer.

You stole my porridge, said a small bear.

And you tasted mine, said a big male bear.

And mine, said a female bear.

The police officer said, That is theft.

She asked Goldilocks, What about the chair? Did you break it?

Yes, I'm afraid I did said Goldilocks But it was an accident.

It's still criminal damage said the police officer.

It was my chair said another voice. It was the voice of a baby bear. He said, I liked my chair. Now I have no chair.

The male bear said, She slept in my wife's bed too.

You'll have to come with us to the police station said the police officer.

Subject knowledge

1. Preliminary notes about grammar

Grammar involves the way in which words of different types are combined into sentences. The explanatory sections that follow will include definitions of types of word along with notes on how they are combined into sentences.

Three preliminary points about grammar:

- Function is all-important. Where a word is placed in relation to another word is crucial in deciding whether it is functioning as a verb or a noun. For example, the word 'run' will often be thought of as a verb. However, in a sentence like *They went for a run*, the word functions as a noun and the verb is 'went'.
- There are some consistencies in the way spelling is linked to grammar. For example, words like 'play' and 'shout' have the 'ed' ending to make past tense verbs, 'played' and 'shouted'. Adjectives like 'quick' and 'slow' take a 'ly' ending to make adverbs like 'quickly' and 'slowly'. There are exceptions to these rules but such consistencies can still prove useful when it comes to understanding the grammar of sentences.
- Nothing is sacred in language. Rules change over time; the double negative has gained currency, and regional variation in accent and dialect is now far more valued than has been the case in the past. The rules of grammar that follow are subject to change as the language we use lives and grows.

2. Words and functions

Grammar picks out the functions of words. The major classes or types of word in the English language are:

Noun

The name of something or someone, including concrete things, such as 'dog' or 'tree', and abstract things, such as 'happiness' or 'fear'.

Pronoun

A word that replaces a noun. The noun 'John' in *John is ill* can be replaced by a pronoun 'he', making *He is ill.*

Verb

A word that denotes an action or a happening. In the sentence *I ate the cake* the verb is 'ate'. These are sometimes referred to as 'doing' words.

Adjective

A word that modifies a noun. In the phrase *the little boat* the adjective 'little' describes the noun 'boat'.

Adverb
A word that modifies a verb. In the phrase *he slowly walked* the adverb is 'slowly'.

Preposition
A word or phrase that shows the relationship of one thing to another. In the phrase *the house beside the sea* the preposition 'beside' places the two nouns in relation to each other.

Conjunction
A word or phrase that joins other words and phrases. A simple example is the word 'and' that joins nouns in *Snow White and Doc and Sneezy.*

Determiner
Determiners appear before nouns and denote whether the noun is specific (*give me the book*) or not (*give me a book*). Note that 'the' (definite article) and 'a' or 'an' (indefinite articles) are the most common types of determiner.

Interjection
A word or phrase expressing or exclaiming an emotion, such as 'Oh!' and 'Aaargh!'
The various word types can be found in the following example sentences:

Lou	saw	his	new	house	from	the	train.
noun	verb	pronoun	adjective	noun	preposition	article	noun
Yeow!	I	hit	my	head	on	the	door.
interjection	pronoun	verb	pronoun	noun	preposition	article	noun
Amir	sadly	lost	his	bus fare	down	the	drain.
noun	adverb	verb	pronoun	noun	preposition	article	noun
Give	Jan	a	good	book	for	her	birthday.
verb	noun	article	adjective	noun	conjunction	pronoun	noun

The pages that follow provide more information on these word classes.

Nouns
There are four types of noun in English.

A **noun** is the name of someone or something.

Common nouns are general names for things. For example, in the sentence *I fed the dog*, the noun 'dog' could be used to refer to any dog, not to a specific one. Other examples include 'boy', 'country', 'book', 'apple'.

Proper nouns are the specific names given to identify things or people. In a phrase like *Sam is my dog* the word 'dog' is the common noun but 'Sam' is a proper noun because it refers to and identifies a specific dog. Other examples include 'Wales' and 'Amazing Grace'.

Collective nouns refer to a group of things together, such as 'a flock (of sheep)' or 'a bunch (of bananas)'.

Abstract nouns refer to things that are not concrete, such as an action, a concept, an event, quality or state. Abstract nouns like 'happiness' and 'fulfilment' refer to ideas or feelings which are non-countable; others, such as 'hour', 'joke' and 'quantity' are countable.

Nouns can be singular or plural. To change a singular to a plural the usual rule is to add 's'. This table includes other rules to bear in mind:

If the singular ends in:	Rule	Examples
'y' after a consonant	Remove 'y', add 'ies'	party → parties
'y' after a vowel	add 's'	donkey → donkeys
'o' after a consonant	add 'es'	potato → potatoes
'o' after a vowel	add 's'	video → videos
an 's' sound such as 's', 'sh', 'x', 'z'	add 'es'	kiss → kisses dish → dishes
a 'ch' sound such as 'ch' or 'tch'	add 'es'	watch → watches church → churches

Pronouns

There are different classes of pronoun. These are the main types:

A **pronoun** is a word that stands in for a noun.

Personal pronouns refer to people or things, such as 'I', 'you', 'it'. The personal pronouns distinguish between subject and object case ('I/me', 'he/him', 'she/her', 'we/us', 'they/them' and the archaic 'thou/thee').

Reflexive pronouns refer to people or things that are also the subject of the sentence. In the sentence *You can do this yourself* the pronoun 'yourself' refers to 'you'. Such pronouns end with 'self' or 'selves'. Other examples include 'myself', 'themselves'.

Possessive pronouns identify people or things as belonging to a person or thing. For example, in the sentence *The book is hers* the possessive pronoun 'hers' refers to 'the book'. Other examples include 'its' and 'yours'. Note that possessive pronouns never take an apostrophe.

Relative pronouns link relative clauses to their nouns. In the sentence *The man who was in disguise sneaked into the room* the relative clause 'who was in disguise' provides extra information about 'the man'. This relative clause is linked by the relative pronoun 'who'. Other examples include 'whom', 'which' and 'that'.

Interrogative pronouns are used in questions. They refer to the thing that is being asked about. In the question *What is your name?* and *Where is the book?* the pronouns 'what' and 'where' stand for the answers – the name and the location of the book.

Demonstrative pronouns are pronouns that 'point'. They are used to show the relation of the speaker to an object. There are four demonstrative pronouns in English 'this', 'that', 'these', 'those' used as in *This is my house* and *That is your house*. They have specific uses, depending upon the position of the object to the speaker:

	Near to speaker	**Far away from speaker**
Singular	this	that
Plural	these	those

Indefinite pronouns stand in for an indefinite noun. The indefinite element can be the number of elements or the nature of them but they are summed up in ambiguous pronouns such as 'any', 'some' or 'several'. Other examples are the pronouns that end with 'body', 'one' and 'thing', such as 'somebody', 'everyone' and 'anything'.

Person

Personal, reflexive and possessive pronouns can be in the first, second or third person.

- First-person pronouns ('I', 'we') involve the speaker or writer.
- Second-person pronouns ('you') refer to the listener or reader.
- Third-person pronouns refer to something other than these two participants in the communication ('he', 'she', 'it', 'they').

The person of the pronoun will agree with particular forms of verbs: 'I like'/'she likes'.

Verbs

A **verb** is a word that denotes an action or a happening.

The **tense** of a verb places a happening in time. The main tenses are the present and past.

English does not have a discrete future tense. It is made in a compound form using a present tense ('I will', 'I shall' and so on) and an infinitive (for example *I will go to the shops*).

The regular past tense is formed by the addition of the suffix 'ed', although some of the most common verbs in English have irregular past tenses.

Present tense (happening now)	**Past tense (happened in past)**	**Future (to happen in future)**
am, say, find, kick	was, said, found, kicked	will be, will say, shall find, shall kick

Continuous verbs

The present participle form of a verb is used to show a continuous action. Whereas a past tense like 'kicked' denotes an action that happened ('I kicked'), the present participle denotes the action as happening and continuing as it is described (*I was kicking*, the imperfect tense, or *I am kicking*, the present continuous). There is a sense in these uses of an action that has not ended.

The present participle usually ends in 'ing', such as 'walking', 'finding', and continuous verbs are made with a form of the verb 'be', such as 'was' or 'am': *I was running* and *I am running*.

Auxiliary verbs

Auxiliary verbs 'help' other verbs – they regularly accompany full verbs, always preceding them in a verb phrase. The auxiliary verbs in English can be divided into three categories:

Primary verbs are used to indicate the timing of a verb, such as 'be', 'have' or 'did' (including all their variations such as 'was', 'were', 'has', 'had' and so on). These can be seen at work in verb forms like *I was watching a film, He has finished eating, I didn't lose my keys*.

Modal verbs indicate the possibility of an action occurring or the necessity of it happening, such as *I might watch a film*, *I should finish eating* and *I shouldn't lose my keys*.

The modal verbs in English are: 'would', 'could', 'might', 'should', 'can', 'will', 'shall', 'may', and 'must'. These verbs never function on their own as main verbs. They always act as auxiliaries helping other verbs.

Marginal modals, namely 'dare', 'need', 'ought to' and 'used to'. These act as modals, such as in the sentences *I dared enter the room*, *You need to go away* and *I ought to eat my dinner*, but they can also act as main verbs, as in *I need cake*.

Adjectives

An **adjective** is a word that modifies a noun.

The main function of adjectives is to define quality or quantity. Examples of the use of descriptions of quality include 'good story', 'sad day' and 'stupid dog'. Examples of the use of descriptions of quantity include 'some stories', 'ten days' and 'many dogs'.

Adjectives can appear in one of three different degrees of intensity. In the table below it can be seen that there are 'er' and 'est' endings that show an adjective is comparative or superlative, though, there are exceptions. The regular comparative is formed by the addition of the suffix 'er' to shorter words and 'more' to longer words ('kind/kinder', 'beautiful/more beautiful'). The regular superlative is formed by the addition of the suffix 'est' to shorter words and 'most' to longer words. Note, however, that some common adjectives are irregular.

Nominative The nominative is the plain form that describes a noun.	**Comparative** The comparative implies a comparison between the noun and something else.	**Superlative** The superlative is the ultimate degree of a particular quality.
Examples	**Examples**	**Examples**
long	longer	longest
small	smaller	smallest
big	bigger	biggest
fast	faster	fastest
bad	worse	worst
good	better	best
far	farther/further	farthest/furthest

> An **adverb** is a word that modifies a verb.

Adverbs

Adverbs provide extra information about the time, place or manner in which the action of a verb happened.

Manner Provides information about the manner in which the action was done.	Ali *quickly* ran home. The cat climbed *fearfully* up the tree.
Time Provides information about the time at which the action occurred.	*Yesterday* Ali ran home. *Sometimes* the cat climbed up the tree.
Place Provides information about where the action took place.	*Outside* Ali ran home. *In the garden* the cat climbed up the tree.

Variations in the degree of intensity of an adverb are indicated by other adjectives such as 'very', 'rather', 'quite' and 'somewhat'. Comparative forms include 'very quickly', 'rather slowly', and 'most happily'.

The majority of single-word adverbs are made by adding 'ly' to an adjective: 'quick/quickly', 'slow/slowly' and so on.

> A **preposition** is a word or phrase that shows the relationship of one thing to another.

Prepositions

Prepositions show how nouns or pronouns are positioned in relation to other nouns and pronouns in the same sentence. This can often be the location of one thing in relation to another in space, such as 'on', 'over', 'near'; or time, such as 'before', 'after'.

Prepositions are usually placed before a noun. They can consist of one word (*The cat* in *the tree*...), two words (*The cat* close to *the gate*...) or three (*The cat* on top of *the roof*...).

> A **determiner** identifies whether a noun is known or unknown.

Determiners

There are different types of determiner:

Articles are the most common type: 'the' (definite article) and 'a' or 'an' (indefinite article).

Possessives are often possessive pronouns such as 'my', 'your', 'our', but can also be nouns with an apostrophe, with or without an 's' (as in *Jane's car, the Prime Minister's speech, the girls' results*.)

Demonstratives are used to show the relation of the speaker to an object. There are four demonstrative pronouns in English 'this', 'that', 'these', 'those'. (See page 150.)

Quantifiers are used to express the quantity of a noun, for example: (indefinite quantity) 'some', 'many', 'several'; (definite quantity) 'every', 'both', 'all', 'four', 'seventy'.

Connectives

The job of a connective is to maintain cohesion through a piece of text.

A **connective** is a word or phrase that links clauses or sentences.

Connectives can be:

- Conjunctions – connect clauses within one sentence.
- Connecting adverbs – connect ideas in separate sentences.

Conjunctions

Conjunctions are a special type of connective. There are two types: coordinating and subordinating.

Coordinating conjunctions connect clauses of equal weight. For example: *I like cake and I like tea.* Coordinating conjunctions include: 'and', 'but', 'or' and 'so'.

Subordinating conjunctions are used where the clauses of unequal weight, they begin a subordinate clause. For example: *The dog barked because he saw the burglar.* Subordinating conjunctions include: 'because', 'when', 'while', 'that', 'although', 'if', 'until', 'after', before' and 'since'.

Name of conjunction	Nature of conjunction	Examples
Addition	One or more clause together	We had our tea *and* went out to play.
Opposition	One or more clauses in opposition	I like coffee *but* my brother hates it. It could rain *or* it could snow.
Time	One or more clauses connected over time	Toby had his tea *then* went out to play. The bus left *before* we reached the stop.
Cause	One or more clauses causing or caused by another	I took a map *so that* we wouldn't get lost. We got lost *because* we had the wrong map.

Connecting adverbs

The table below provides the function of the adverbs and examples of the type of words used for that purpose.

Addition	'also', 'furthermore', 'moreover', 'likewise'
Opposition	'however', 'never the less', 'on the other hand'
Time	'just then', 'meanwhile', 'later'
Result	'therefore', 'as a result'
Reinforcing	'besides', 'anyway'
Explaining	'for example', 'in other words'
Listing	'first of all', 'finally'

3. Understanding sentences

Types of sentence

The four main types of sentence are declarative, interrogative, imperative and exclamatory. The function of a sentence has an effect on the word order; imperatives, for example, often begin with a verb.

Sentence type	Function	Examples
Declarative	Makes a statement	The house is down the lane. Joe rode the bike.
Interrogative	Asks a question	Where is the house? What is Joe doing?
Imperative	Issues a command or direction	Turn left at the traffic lights. Get on your bike!
Exclamatory	Issues an interjection	Wow, what a mess! Oh no!

Sentences: Clauses and complexities

Phrases

A phrase is a set of words performing a grammatical function. In the sentence *The little, old, fierce dog brutally chased the sad and fearful cat*, there are three distinct units performing grammatical functions. The first phrase in this sentence essentially names the dog and provides descriptive information. This is a noun phrase, performing the job of a noun – 'the little, old, fierce dog'. To do this the phrase uses adjectives.

The important thing to look out for is the way in which words build around a key word in a phrase. So here the words 'little', 'old' and 'fierce' are built around the word 'dog'. In examples like these, 'dog' is referred to as the **headword** and the adjectives are termed **modifiers**. Together, the modifier and headword make up the noun phrase. Modifiers can also come after the noun, as in *The little, old, fierce dog that didn't like cats brutally chased the sad and fearful cat*. In this example 'little, 'old' and 'fierce' are **premodifiers** and the phrase 'that didn't like cats' is a **postmodifier**. The noun phrase is just one of the types of phrase that can be made.

Phrase type	Examples
Noun phrase	The *little, old fierce dog* didn't like cats. She gave him *a carefully and colourfully covered book*.
Verb phrase	The dog *had been hiding* in the house. The man *climbed through* the window without a sound.
Adjectival phrase	The floor was *completely clean*. The floor was *so clean you could eat your dinner off it*.
Adverbial phrase	I finished my lunch *very slowly indeed*. *More confidently than usual*, she entered the room.
Prepositional phrase	The cat sat *at the top of* the tree. The phone rang *in the middle of* the night.

Notice that phrases can appear within phrases. A noun phrase like 'carefully and colourfully covered book' contains the adjectival phrase 'carefully and colourfully covered'. This string of words forms the adjectival phrase in which the words 'carefully' and 'colourfully' modify the adjective 'covered'. Together these words, 'carefully and colourfully covered', modify the noun 'book', creating a distinct noun phrase. This is worth noting as it shows how the boundaries between phrases can be blurred – a fact that can cause confusion unless borne in mind!

Clauses

Clauses are units of meaning included within a sentence, usually containing a verb and other elements linked to it. *The burglar ran* is a clause containing the definite article, noun and verb; *The burglar quickly ran from the little house* is also a clause that adds an adverb, preposition and adjective. The essential element in a clause is the verb. Clauses look very much like small sentences – indeed sentences can be constructed of just one clause: *The burglar hid*, *I like cake*.

Sentences can also be constructed out of a number of clauses linked together: *The burglar ran and I chased him because he stole my cake*. This sentence contains three clauses: 'The burglar ran', 'I chased him', 'he stole my cake'.

Clauses and phrases: the difference

Clauses include participants in an action denoted by a verb. Phrases, however, need not necessarily contain a verb. These phrases make little sense on their own: 'without a sound', 'very slowly indeed'. They work as part of a clause.

Simple, compound and complex sentences

The addition of clauses to single-clause sentences (simple sentences) can make multi-clause sentences (complex or compound sentences).

Simple sentences are made up of one clause, for example: *The dog barked*, *Sam was scared*.

Compound sentences are made up of clauses added to clauses. In compound sentences each of the clauses is of equal value; no clause is dependent on another. An example of a compound sentence is: *The dog barked and the parrot squawked*. Both these clauses are of equal importance: 'The dog barked', 'the parrot squawked'. Other compound sentences include, for example: *I like coffee and I like chocolate*, *I like coffee, but I don't like tea*.

Complex sentences are made up of a main clause with a subordinate clause or clauses. Subordinate clauses make sense in relation to the main clause. They say something about it and are dependent upon it, such as in the sentences: *The dog barked because he saw a burglar*; *Sam was scared so he phoned the police*.

In both these cases the subordinate clause ('he saw a burglar', 'he phoned the police') is elaborating on the main clause. They explain why the dog barked or why Sam was scared and, in doing so, are subordinate to those actions. The reader needs to see the main clauses to fully appreciate what the subordinate ones are stating.

Subject and object

The **subject** of a sentence or clause is the agent that performs the action denoted by the verb – *Shaun threw the ball*. The **object** is the agent to which the verb is done – 'ball'. It could be said that the subject does the verb to the object (a simplification but a useful one). The simplest type of sentence is known as the SVO (subject–verb–object) sentence (or clause), as in *You lost your way*, *I found the book* and *Lewis met Chloe*.

The active voice and the passive voice

These contrast two ways of saying the same thing:

Active voice	Passive voice
I found the book. Megan met Ben. The cow jumped over the moon.	The book was found by me. Ben was met by Megan. The moon was jumped over by the cow.

The two types of clause put the same subject matter in a different voice. Passive clauses are made up of a subject and verb followed by an agent.

The book	was found by	me.
subject	verb	agent
Ben	was met by	Megan.
subject	verb	agent

Sentences can be written in the active or the passive voice. A sentence can be changed from the active to the passive voice by:

- moving the subject to the end of the clause
- moving the object to the start of the clause
- changing the verb or verb phrase by placing a form of the verb 'be' before it (as in 'was found')
- changing the verb or verb phrase by placing 'by' after it.

In passive clauses the agent can be deleted, either because it does not need mentioning or because a positive choice is made to omit it. Texts on science may leave out the agent, with sentences such as *The water is added to the salt and stirred*.

4. Punctuation

Punctuation provides marks within sentences that guide the reader. Speech doesn't need punctuation (and would sound bizarre if it included noises for full stops and so on). In speech, much is communicated by pausing, changing tone and so on. In writing, the marks within and around a sentence provide indications of when to pause, when something is being quoted and so on.

Punctuation	Uses	Examples
A	**Capital letter** 1. Starts a sentence. 2. Indicates proper nouns. 3. Emphasises certain words.	1. All I want is cake. 2. You can call me Al. 3. I want it TOMORROW!
.	**Full stop** Ends sentences that are not questions or exclamations.	This is a sentence.
?	**Question mark** Ends a sentence that is a question.	Is this a question?
!	**Exclamation mark** Ends a sentence that is an exclamation.	Don't do that!
" " ' '	**Inverted commas (or quotation/ speech marks)** Encloses direct speech. Can be double or single.	"Help me," the man yelled. 'Help me,' the man yelled.
,	**Comma** 1. Places a pause between clauses within a sentence. 2. Separates items in a list. 3. Separates adjectives in a series. 4. Completely encloses clauses inserted in a sentence. 5. Marks speech from words denoting who said them.	1. We were late, although it didn't matter. 2. You will need eggs, butter and flour. 3. I wore a long, green, frilly skirt. 4. We were, after we had rushed to get there, late for the film. 5. 'Thank you,' I said.
-	**Hyphen** Connects elements of certain words.	Re-read, south-west.
:	**Colon** 1. Introduces lists (including examples). 2. Introduces summaries. 3. Introduces (direct) quotations. 4. Introduces a second clause that expands or illustrates the meaning of the first.	1. To go skiing these are the main items you will need: a hat, goggles, gloves and sunscreen. 2. We have learned the following on the ski slope: do a snow plough to slow down. 3. My instructor always says: 'Bend those knees.' 4. The snow hardened: it turned into ice.

Punctuation	Uses	Examples
;	**Semicolon** 1. Separates two closely linked clauses, and shows there is a link between them. 2. Separates items in a complex list.	1. On Tuesday, the bus was late; the train was early. 2. You can go by aeroplane, train and taxi; Channel tunnel train, coach, then a short walk; or aeroplane and car.
'	**Apostrophe of possession** Denotes the ownership of one thing by another (see page 159).	This is Mona's scarf. These are the teachers' books.
'	**Apostrophe of contraction** Shows the omission of a letter(s) when two (or occasionally more) words are contracted.	Don't walk on the grass.
...	**Ellipsis** 1. Shows the omission of words. 2. Indicates a pause.	1. The teacher moaned, 'Look at this floor... a mess... this class...' 2. Lou said: 'I think I locked the door... no, hang on, did I?'
( )	**Brackets** Contains a parenthesis – a word or phrase added to a sentence to give a bit more information.	The cupboard (which had been in my family for years) was broken.
–	**Dash** 1. Indicates additional information, with more emphasis than a comma. 2. Indicates a pause, especially for effect at the end of a sentence. 3. Contains extra information (used instead of brackets).	1. She is a teacher – and a very good one too. 2. We all know what to expect – the worst. 3. You finished that job – and I don't know how – before the deadline.

Adding an apostrophe of possession

The addition of an apostrophe can create confusion. The main thing to look at is the noun – ask:

- Is it singular or plural?
- Does it end in an 's'?

If the noun is singular and doesn't end in 's', you add an apostrophe and an 's', for example: *Indra's house* *the firefighter's bravery*	**If the noun is singular and ends in 's'**, you add an apostrophe and an 's', for example: *the bus's wheels* *Thomas's pen*
If the noun is plural and doesn't end in 's', you add an apostrophe and an 's', for example: *the women's magazine* *the geese's flight*	**If the noun is plural and ends in 's'**, you add an apostrophe but don't add an 's', for example: *the boys' clothes* *the dancers' performance*